D0392395

REGULATORS GONE WILD

REGULATORS GONE WILD

HOW THE EPA IS RUINING AMERICAN INDUSTRY

RICH TRZUPEK

Encounter Books New York • London

First American edition published in 2011 by Encounter Books,
an activity of Encounter for Culture and Education, Inc.,
a nonprofit, tax exempt corporation.
Encounter Books website address: www.encounterbooks.com

Manufactured in the United States and printed on
acid-free paper. The paper used in this publication meets
the minimum requirements of ANSI/NISO Z39.48 1992
(R 1997) (*Permanence of Paper*).

FIRST AMERICAN EDITION

LIBRARY OF CONGRESS CATALOGING-IN-PUBLICATION DATA
Trzupek, Rich.
Regulators gone wild: how the EPA is ruining American industry/
by Rich Trzupek.
p. cm.
Includes bibliographical references and index.
ISBN-13: 978-1-59403-526-5 (hardcover: alk. paper)
ISBN-10: 1-59403-526-1 (hardcover : alk. paper) 1. Environmental man-
agement—United States. 2. Environmental policy—United States. 3. Indus-
tries—Environmental aspects—United States. 4. Pollution—Government
policy—United States. 5. Factory and trade waste—Government policy—United
States. 6. United States. Environmental Protection Agency. I. Title.
GE310.T79 2011

363.700973—dc22

2010038081

Dedication

*For Walter Trzupek, a man of honor who sweated in the mills
for thirty-five years to raise six children. I miss you, Dad.*

CONTENTS

FOREWORD

WHEN RICH TRZUPEK ASKED ME TO WRITE THE foreword to his book, he had no idea how much of a role I unintentionally played in the horror story created by the United States Environmental Protection Agency (USEPA) that is so eloquently described in this book. Environmental Regulations have stifled American Enterprise. I feel great personal guilt for having aided and abetted the establishment of the USEPA in 1971, when I was an unpaid consultant to government. Forty years ago there was pressing need take action, because few understood how badly we had been mistreating our environment. Yet, the public would soon learn the lesson, and the need for overbearing regulations would decline dramatically. In the late 1970s, America became environmentally conscious. Suddenly aware of our surroundings, people everywhere understood how important it was to bequeath all the beauty of nature to our children and to their children. Unfortunately that awareness came too late to stem the tide of strangling unnecessary regulations. The die was cast, and an agency was born capable of expanding its manpower and annual budget simply by turning every potential anthill of fear into a mountain of hysteria. Today it is no exaggeration to say that virtually any environmental ill that attracts media attention is distorted at least an order of magnitude in order to frighten an unwitting and scientifically untrained public.

Rich Trzupek tells us that forty years ago environmental regulation was about protecting and preserving nature, but in this century it has become something very different. Modern environmental regulation is a game that has little or nothing to do with preserving our resources. We have truly cleaned up the developed world, transforming the average American and most business persons into concerned citizens in the process. This was once the goal of Sierra Clubs, Environmental Defense Funds, and Natural Resource Defense Councils, but that is not the case today. The transformation in corporate ethics and improvement in environmental quality no longer seem to matter to these groups. They demand more and more action and create more and more crises in order to raise funds, either by creating fear where none should exist or by shamelessly exploiting real human tragedies like the Gulf oil spill in the summer of 2010.

No nation has a more exemplary record of cleaning and then protecting its environment than the United States, but today's environmental groups are determined to hide these facts so they can keep the money flowing and expand their power even further. They say they celebrate an annual Earth Day, but they do no such thing. They wring their hands each April 22 over the destruction of Mother Earth that they ascribe to mankind, and then pretend that we haven't made any progress at all.

Whenever we achieve reasonable air- and water-quality goals, environmental lobbyists convince the USEPA to lower the standards so they can claim our environment is declining. As a result, more air-sheds and watersheds are defined as being out of compliance with the rules—if not with reality. The USEPA has become the coconspirator of the fabulously wealthy and powerful environmental lobby, which calls the shots and essentially pays the bloated salaries of the ever-expanding government workforce.

They warmed up the battle to enslave society to unreasonable environmental standards by floating fallacies about man's impact on a nonexistent ozone hole. Then they hit a grand slam when they discovered that the entire world could be held captive under the completely unsubstantiated idea that man could effectively affect his climate for either good or evil.

Although the bulk of the folks working in the government/environment scare complex are in it for the money, a clear socialist element has also crept in, using eco-machinations to inhibit economic growth, destroy capitalism, and create a more collectivist society. Even as society loses in general, Trzupek tells the poignant stories of the well-meaning people caught in the web of a regulatory machine that is no longer of value to society. He explains that it is the small to midsize businesses—the bedrock of our economy strength that pay most dearly. They struggle to do the right thing, but the system is so complex that it is difficult to know what the right thing is. They are trapped in fine print by regulators who are not protecting the environment, "but who have grown skillful at creating the kinds of pointless profitable snares that personal-injury lawyers would envy."

It is my very strong personal opinion that as radical as it may seem, USEPA should be disbanded and its duties and responsibilities given over to our fifty state EPAs, which are are more than capable of doing the job and far more sensitive to the needs of their state's citizens. If past experience is any guide, the states will be vigilant in fulfilling their mandate to protect their native resources.

My opinion is motivated in part by the incredibly poor science USEPA uses to set standards for chemicals in our environment. They rely upon badly designed rodent studies, which in turn depend on the ability to draw strong comparisons between mice, men, and mathematical models based on single experiments that are never repeated. For example, we know that lead has no redeeming qualities in human physiology, but USEPA assumes further that lead paint in inner city neighborhoods accounts for poor grades of young students, while they ignore the role that poverty plays in academic achievement.

USEPA's real money machine is its enforcement of the Comprehensive Environmental Response, Compensation, and Liability Act, which we know as CERCLA. This act, which was initially eighty-seven pages long, holds everyone involved in a pollution case wholly liable for all the cleanup of the pollution found, even if an individual or firm contributed but a thimble full of contaminant. It's called joint and severable liability in legal terms, and it has sent many a company into bankruptcy.

Things have now gone from bad to worse as President Obama has installed a triumvirate of environmental policymakers: Lisa Jackson, Carol Browner, and Steven Chu, whose radical approach to power over the public is beyond anything we have seen before. This administration is pushing an unprecedanted radical environmental agenda, and especially in light of this fact, Trzupek's book is vital. Everyone concerned about making America prosperous again should read it. Of course, not everyone will read it, but *you* are reading it, and you can carry its message to your friends and neighbors and associates. Environmental regulations have indeed gone wild.

Dr. Jay Lehr
The Heartland Institute

COMPETITION AMIDST CONFUSION

ENVIRONMENTAL REGULATIONS ARE NOT ALWAYS about environmental protection. Today, more than ever, regulations seem to have been designed by accountants rather than by scientists. The focus is on the nth decimal place and super-fluous sets of overlapping records. Actual impacts on the environment fade into the background. Few seem to realize that the country has grown, and continues to grow, cleaner every year. Much of the public believes that the planet is dying and that industry is, therefore, responsible for the crime. Accordingly, regulators look for increasingly more obscure means to punish supposed transgressors. In the absence of any actual damage to the environment, they are content to turn the slightest misdemeanor into the ecological equivalent of homicide. Consider the strange but sadly representative case of Norwood Marking Systems.

Norwood Marking Systems is a small company located in the small town of Frankfort, Illinois. Employing about fifty people, Norwood produces coated plastic film used in price-labeling machinery, one of those innocuous products that no one notices although everyone utilizes it each day.

The production process involves solvents, which can contaminate the air. As responsible members of the community, the company purchased, and duly permitted, an incinerator that destroyed the offending fumes. They kept the records that the Environmental Protection Agency (EPA) demanded. They filed all their environmental reports on time. They monitored the incinerator, per EPA guidelines, to make sure it was always doing its job. Furthermore, they never emitted more pollutants than the law allowed.

Nonetheless, the company still managed to run afoul of the agency. Back in the early 1990s, the USEPA issued new rules requiring an official certification, in which each company verified that it was following every applicable EPA rule. Norwood failed to notice the new requirement, which is understandable given the myriad of regulations that might apply to a company at any given moment on the local, state, and federal levels. The volume of paper these agencies generate each year challenges even the largest and most sophisticated corporate environmental staff. At Norwood's level, it takes a tremendous effort to keep up.

Thus, when the official notice of violation arrived, the company, knowing it had complied, was not worried. It had kept its records and filed its reports. Most important, it was not polluting more than it should. Norwood was and is one of the good guys. The company merely had failed to file some obscure piece of paper that confirmed those facts. Norwood would correct the oversight and move on. Surely, the EPA would not feel the need to administer any punishment.

Norwood was wrong. Its control device itself was not enough. Its permit was not enough. The records, the reports, the monitoring, the maintenance logs, and all the best operational practices were not enough. In the EPA's world, one more piece of paper is always needed. USEPA sued the company for violations of the Clean Air Act. No one disputed the fact that Norwood was doing the right thing. Its crime was failing to inform the right number of bureaucrats.

The feds sued, demanding over $100,000 in penalties for the transgression. The company fought back, reducing the fine to $40,000 before finally surrendering to the bureaucratic juggernaut. The ultimate effect on the environment? None. Uncle Sam did pretty well, though.

Even companies that do not get caught in the snares of arbitrary environmental enforcement have it tough. Being a manufacturer in America these days is not easy: money is tight, customers demand perfection, and the challenge of twenty-cents-per-hour labor in China frightens every entrepreneur paying a hundred times that rate. Let us look at another company in the same line of business and their struggles with the EPA. Nestled in the quiet, far-northern suburbs of Chicago, Vonco Products is a company that has managed not only to survive, but thrive. It has done so by sticking to a classically American script featuring innovation, service, and speed to beat their competition.

Nonetheless, the biggest threat to this company may not be competitors at home and abroad, but the faceless regulators who stifle the mobility and creativity of Vonco and thousands of other American businesses. All must somehow find ways to deal with the volume of excessive and unnecessary environmental regulation that goes far beyond addressing society's actual needs. Environmental regulation is, of course, only one of the many ways that bureaucrats choke industry; but in a world where everyone is expected to "go green"—even though few understand why they are supposed to do so or how—it is an increasingly important and costly part of the big-government equation.

Vonco started out making plastic bags in 1955, when the process was a cheap, easy segment of the printing industry production. One bought plastic on giant rolls, cut it square, performed some minor fabrication, laid down some graphics, and merrily counted the profits. Over the years, the task would evolve into something much more complicated. The companies who bought the product eventually wanted more than simple bags. Classy printing, just-in-time delivery, and unusual shapes eventually became a big part of the market. Cheaper bags, with less quality and sizzle, developed into the second half of the industry: a fiercely competitive commodity market.

Some bag producers managed to keep up. Many did not. Revenue in the printing industry steadily dropped over the years, falling more than 25 percent from its peak in 1989. Between 1997 and 2006, more than 150,000 jobs disappeared in the printing industry. That is over 20 percent of all printing-industry employment lost, a far greater rate than that of the overall economy in the same period. Furthermore, this loss occurred *before* the onset of the Great Recession. Advances in electronic forms of communication are responsible for some of that decline, but these statistics also reflect both the volume of imports and the number of American printers who tried—and failed—to play the low end of the market, only to be beaten by cheap labor available in Mexico and overseas.

A trio of determined owners kept Vonco going in this competitive environment. They realized that survival meant something more clever than business as usual. They focused on the high-end of the market. Unusually shaped bags and balloons became their specialty. If a customer needed an oddly shaped cut to match his oddly shaped floor sweeper, or wanted an inflatable "We're Number One" finger, Vonco could build a machine to produce it in quantity and with high quality.

Vonco also invented Thunderstix®, the ubiquitous, inflatable noisemakers that frenzied fans bang together during all sorts of sporting events. Vonco's vice president and general manager John LaRoi, an energetic, tireless, middle-aged father of five, developed and patented the one-way pneumatic valve that makes Thunderstix® possible. His design allowed fans to inflate the noisemakers easily, letting air in without allowing it to escape after blowing into the tube had stopped. Moreover, he designed Thunderstix® so that it is impossible to overinflate the product.

Competitors overseas were not overly worried about details such as patents, and they quickly copied Vonco's design, offering imitations at prices the company could not possibly match. This turn of events was troubling, but Vonco's strategy—to focus on quality and service—would be justified in the end. "We lost some business for a while," LaRoi said. "But almost all of it came back. The other guys were offering their stuff cheap, but they couldn't match our delivery. It takes at least two or three weeks to make something in China and ship it here. If you've got a play-off game next week, you don't have that kind of time. We've filled orders in less than forty-eight hours when we've had to. Plus, a lot of customers noticed that the quality just wasn't there. Even if they have more time, they're willing to pay a little extra for something that's printed right."

That sort of attitude and focus—combined with an enthusiastic workforce, family atmosphere, and aggressive leadership—allowed Vonco to expand its operations. In 2003, the company added 20,000 square feet of floor space and two more printing presses to its operation.

Increasing its fleet of printing presses to three also meant that Vonco might have increased its emissions of printing-ink solvents. Those solvents, generically called volatile organic compounds (VOCs), are closely regulated by the U.S. and Illinois EPAs. VOCs contribute to the formation of ground-level ozone. The EPA is a big fan of ozone in the upper atmosphere, where it helps shield us from the sun's dangerous rays, but it frowns upon ozone in that portion of the atmosphere where people breathe. Ground-level ozone is the biggest part of what most of us call smog, the brown haze that hangs over large cities on hot summer days. Smog reduction has been a primary focus of the EPA for decades, with breathing problems among the very young, very old, and asthmatics of all ages being the reasons most often cited for cutting ozone concentrations.

Fortunately, for the very young, the very old, and asthmatics, Vonco's growth meant that it actually had to reduce its solvent emissions. State and federal rules dictated that the company had to spend several hundred thousand dollars to collect and destroy the offending chemicals. Even though it would be increasing its capacity to three printing presses, its emissions would actually go down. That might have been the end of it, if the issue were actually about pollution. It was not. In today's world, pollution control too often takes a backseat to paperwork.

Before the company could install the new presses and the new incinerator to destroy the offending fumes, Vonco had to file for a construction permit. The EPA then took a few months to approve the application before the company could finally purchase its emissions-control device. "Fair enough," some would say, although the attendant delay can often be longer than many fast-moving entrepreneurs would be able to tolerate. However, a permit to build marked only the beginning of Vonco's ordeal. Once the permit was issued, Vonco was obliged to spend $10,000 to have the incinerator (these days, the politically correct term is "thermal oxider") tested. Successfully crossing that hurdle, the company then had to refile for an operating permit within 180 days, paying a professional consultant another $10,000 to fill out forms that make the IRS's ubiquitous 1040 seem like tic-tac-toe.

The second permit, in turn, came with a variety of detailed conditions. The company had to track how much ink it used every month, record the temperature at which the incinerator operated, keep a maintenance log on the incinerator and presses, monitor press operating times, calculate the amount of VOCs in each ink, and file a plethora of reports with the EPA. Somewhere in this swamp of busywork hides a bottom line: How much of the bad stuff escaped into the air? That question is ultimately answered by the piles of paper a company like Vonco must maintain, but it is a solitary tree lost in an unending forest of data.

As an intelligent businessman who always wanted to do the right thing, LaRoi understood the game as well as anyone. He dutifully collected the mountain of paperwork the EPA required, carefully compiled against the day when inspectors would invade his business in the hopes of finding some obscure permit condition or regulation with which he had failed to comply. Two-inch binders lined a shelf of his office, labeled for each year that he has collected the numbers the EPA demanded. Over the years, it has become a bigger and bigger part of his job.

"I probably spend an average of twenty hours a month on this stuff," LaRoi said. "Plus there's the time that our guys on the floor put in so I get the data I need." Every May, LaRoi has to tell the EPA what he emitted in the previous year. Each October, he has to file a report that covers emissions during the warm-weather ozone season—May 1 through September 30. July 1 is the deadline for his Form R report, which details what hazardous materials he might have handled. Depending on his operations, he might also have to file hazardous-waste, Tier 2, and wastewater reports.

All of those routine filings—most of which cover the same ground repeatedly while simply employing new forms, different agencies, and more obscure calculations—pale in comparison to what a man like LaRoi faces when and if he should try to expand his business. Let us imagine that Vonco wants to build a brand-new plant. The company's creative, customer-focused approach has built new markets in another part of the country. New sales are at its fingertips. Jobs will be created. How soon can they respond?

Forty years ago, it would have been simple: buy a press, lease some space, hire a few workers, and get rolling. Many printers kept presses in storage back then, ready to install, and they could churn out a product within a week or two of having obtained a contract. Those days are long gone. Regulatory concerns now constrain almost any significant change in manufacturing activity. Since air pollution is involved in bag printing, as it is with most manufacturing processes, an air-pollution construction permit must be secured. In most states, that will take a minimum of ninety days. Depending on the size of the project, it could take a year or longer.

The Army Corps of Engineers must be satisfied that wetlands will not be lost, and the environmental evaluation could take twelve to eighteen months, depending on the region of the country. Storm-water runoff regulations, designed to prevent silt deposits in rivers, must be addressed. Historical preservation agencies have to be convinced that no ancient artifacts will be disturbed. Naturalists can kill the venture if they deem that threatened or endangered species are in peril. The effects on the local wastewater-handling system have to be evaluated. Local municipalities will also look at these issues, along with a dozen more contingents; and they will factor in the reaction of locals who often judge any industrial project as a dangerous invader rather than a benevolent, income-generating job creator and valued member of the host community.

Despite all these rules and the endless piles of paperwork, the myth persists in popular perception: businesses can get away with whatever they want. What may have been true forty years ago is not close to reality today. Inspired by environmental groups that refuse to acknowledge the massive ecological progress we have achieved, encouraged by an ignorant media largely populated by reporters who flunked every science course they might have been forced to take, and abandoned by indifferent politicians, the American public knows no better. In this Age of Fear, people are convinced that the planet is dying and its population is in grave danger. In fact, the exact opposite is true. Until and unless we come to that rational conclusion, ground-breaking, inspiring small businesses such as Vonco will continue to accomplish less than they could.

In the chapters that follow, we will examine how environmental regulation and regulators in America have extended their reach into virtually every facet of our economy over the last forty years. These invasions have little to do with protecting the environment and much to do with preserving the atmosphere of fear that ensures that everyone with a "green job" remains employed. We will look at how toxic risks are wildly inflated by environmental groups and how attorneys and corporations exploit those exaggerations to line their own pockets. We will examine the role that the technically ignorant media play in perpetuating the myth that America is choking in pollution when, in fact, the United States is one of the cleanest nations on earth.

We will consider not only how needlessly intrusive environmental regulation has become, but how often the response of regulators is completely disproportionate to the gravity of the crime. Of course, no study of environmental regulation in America in the twenty-first century would be complete without closely examining the hot-button environmental issue of the day: the proposition that earth's climate is changing in an unprecedented way and that mankind is responsible for this phenomenon. One will probably be surprised to learn that, far from ignoring this supposed problem, the United States has made commitments to drastically reduce fossil fuel use over the next twenty years in ways that few people understand. Finally, we will scrutinize the polices of the most radical USEPA that the America has ever known since that agency was first created: the USEPA that, Lisa Jackson, Barack Obama's choice as administrator is leading.

Forty years ago, environmental regulation was about protecting our health and preserving nature. In the twenty-first century, it has become something far different. Environmental groups turn the smallest risks into the biggest threats, and regulators play right into their hands. Modern environmental regulation is a game, one that usually has little or nothing to do with preserving our resources or the natural order. It is about obscure forms, trip-wire reports, and anal-retentive inspectors. We have cleaned up the world and transformed the average American businessman from an uncaring profiteer into a concerned fellow citizen. Presumably, that transformation was the original goal of the Sierra Clubs, Environmental Defense Funds, and Natural Resource Defense Councils of the world.

Yet a transformation in corporate ethics and a dramatic improvement in environmental quality does not seem to matter to these groups. They constantly demand more. Should an accident occur, such as the 2010 oil spill in the Gulf of Mexico, they will pounce on the disaster, exploiting the tragedy shamelessly to push their agenda. They will always want more, and our representatives on both sides of the political aisle are ever ready to give in to them. It is the concerned American entrepreneur, the bedrock of our success, who pays the price directly. However, if we think about it a moment longer, it becomes clear that we all pay.

CHAPTER ONE

MAKING THE GRADE

W E LIVE LONGER THAN EVER. WE POLLUTE LESS than ever. Need anyone say more?

Since 1970 (the advent of the modern environmental movement), the average life expectancy in the United States has risen from seventy-one to over seventy-seven years. In that time, the amount of pollutants released into the air, water, and soil has dropped precipitously. Given that history, one would think that environmental advocacy groups would be celebrating their accomplishments. If Rachael Carson, author of the classic enviro-frenzy best seller *Silent Spring* were still alive, would the facts not move her to song?

We will never know. Surely today's popular environmental groups, who depend on the unlikely specter of impending doom for their financial health, will be the last to admit that progress has been made. In their world, nothing could be worse than progress.

Perfectly willing to use the worst science, they exploit the slightest ambiguity and sell a gullible, technologically challenged media and public their version of reality. It is not reality at all, but that hardly matters. Yet, when science is involved, politicians on either side of the aisle have also been useful idiots. Let us start with those dirty, rotten polluters who helped create the climate of fear that the professional environmental lobby so cynically exploits today.

The CFC (chlorofluorocarbons) issue is a classic example. Prior to 1990, CFCs were the refrigerants commonly used in air-conditioners and refrigerators and were known generically as "Freon" (though there are many different types of Freon). A popular perception in industry, advanced by the late former Washington governor Dixie Lee Ray among others, was that regulations to protect stratospheric ozone by eliminating Freon were wholly unnecessary. Stratospheric ozone, the ozone in the air at about 30,000 feet, is different from ground-level ozone. At ground level, ozone is bad. It is a part of smog, which may inhibit breathing to some extent among high-risk groups. In the upper atmosphere, ozone is good. It blocks the portion of the sun's rays that can lead to skin cancer. Beginning in the seventies, scientists said that chlorinated compounds were destroying ozone in the upper atmosphere. This destruction, in turn, was creating an ozone hole and endangering our lives. "Hogwash," many in industry said. "There's more chlorine emitted by some volcanoes in a single day than by all of industry in a year. Why should we possibly care?"

Many on the right jumped on the bandwagon. When regulations were proposed that would virtually eliminate the use of Freon, industry lobbyists and sympathetic politicians cried foul. These compounds are far heavier than air, they cried, and, therefore, they cannot even make it up into the upper atmosphere. While she was right far more often than not, the late Governor Ray did her cause a disservice by getting this particular issue wrong. Industry and its supporters among policymakers did no better. They either did not understand the science or did not care. Thus, they managed to reinforce the public perception that the business community could not be trusted when environmental issues are at stake.

That the amount of chlorine emitted by volcanoes vastly exceeds the amount of the element produced by industry is true, but that is not the point. Chlorine, as an element, does not matter. It matters no more than the fact that air is seventy-nine percent nitrogen. Brave a little chemistry with me while I explain what I mean. I will keep the lesson as painless as possible.

By itself, nitrogen is an innocuous element. However, if we combine it with hydrogen and carbon in the right proportions, it can form trinitrotoluene (TNT), which is exceptionally explosive. For any chemist, the compound—not the individual element—matters. In essentially the same way, the amount of the element chlorine that a volcano spews out does not matter a whit. The vast majority of its emission is not in a form that would affect the upper ozone layer. Volcanoes regurgitate chlorine in the form of chlorides, which do not react with ozone to any significant degree. It is chlorine in the form of CFCs that can decimate the ozone layer. Volcanoes do not produce CFCs. Man does.

Similarly, the fact that CFCs are heavier than air makes no difference. Thanks to wind and temperature and other boring physical effects, gases do not separate themselves according to their weight in the atmosphere. If gases did cleanly separate themselves according to their weight, nitrogen and oxygen would perfectly divide into layers, destroying life as we know it. We are all still breathing, so we can safely assume that the laws of physics have not been overturned. Given enough time, gases will evenly mix in the atmosphere, regardless of weight.

The theory that CFCs could reach the upper atmosphere and thus subsequently destroy vast amounts of protective ozone is legitimate. However, this possibility does not prove that this theory is correct, only that it has merit. Both environmental advocates and supporters of industry do all of us a disservice when they attack legitimate theories on spurious grounds. In this case, some industry lobbyists, who had strong, legitimate arguments about a number of other environmental issues, chose propaganda over fact. They stuck to an unscientific narrative: CFCs were supposedly too heavy to reach the upper atmosphere. If they had taken Chemistry 101, they would have known better.

The industrial side has engaged in a lot of that sort of spin-doctoring over the years, especially during the rise of the environmental movement. When the original Clean Air and Clean Water Acts were first proposed in the late sixties, industrial groups decried the exorbitant costs of environmental controls. Although that assertion is increasingly true today, that was not the case in 1970. For the general public, many of whom had to dust off their cars each morning and who hoped their rivers would not catch fire the next day, industrial protests seemed more than a little hollow. Forty years ago, America's environment was in sorry shape, so attempts to quash the cleanup so obviously needed seemed to be another example of robber-baron exploitation.

Those early battles set the tone of the environmental debate for the next forty years. A large portion of the populace came to believe that the industrial sector was untrustworthy. Few people could envision a day when American businesses would be on the ropes, battered by foreign competition, while environmental groups and the mainstream media continued—even though the environmental goals we set for ourselves forty years ago have long since been accomplished—to portray America as one of the most polluted nations on earth. Who would have believed that the time would come when the environment was actually clean and the people dedicated to its protection were more interested in fundraising than natural preservation?

Yet that is where we are today. One would be hard-pressed to find a nation that has done more to clean up its act than the United States. Our environmental programs set the standard for the rest of the world. Many nations even copy our regulations wholesale. We have set tough goals, and time and again, we have achieved them. However, having conquered the ecological battlefield, we have typically tried to do more. Progress only seems to whet our appetite for more progress. If we had a sense of history, we would be satisfied in the outcome. We have accomplished more than we expected.

Contemporary environmental groups never acknowledge those remarkable accomplishments They are so intoxicated by the glory of battle, so sure of victory, and so dependent on monetary support for their self-absorbed, bloated wars that they will never admit they have accomplished anything at all. Each year, we celebrate Earth Day, supposedly dedicated to the wonders of nature. However, what environmental groups have never celebrated on Earth Day are our successful efforts to clean up the air and water. Earth Day should be more properly titled "Doomsday," or perhaps "Guilt Day." The average American has expended a huge amount of time, energy, and money to clean up the environment, but environmental groups never offer them any gratitude

We live longer than ever. We pollute less than ever. Who cares? Certainly not the Environmental Defense Fund or the Sierra Club. Admitting as much would endanger their income sources, including many naive but well-meaning suburban housewives and idealistic junior high students who know no better and who willingly open their checkbooks and volunteer their time.

The enviro-lobbies emphasize industry's past propaganda efforts, campaigns that industry initially used (unsuccessfully) in an attempt to minimize the problems that existed. By wildly exaggerating the slight risks that might remain, these same environmental groups act in much the same manner today. "You know you can't trust anything industry has to say," they say in effect. "Trust us—things are worse than ever." Ironically, the environmental lobby has perfected the tactics that their industrial adversaries pioneered. The Sierra Club's propaganda would be the envy of the spin doctors at the old Tobacco Institute.

Cherry-picking is a popular and effective tactic. Environmental groups often choose a single, ugly fact from a pile of data and present it as the whole story, despite how unrepresentative that fact actually is. They will argue that they are telling only the truth, while they conveniently ignore the whole-truth part of the equation. It is as if they were photographing a beautiful woman and chose to zoom in on the unsightly mole on her left shoulder.

Consider the example of EPA's redesignation of ozone non-attainment areas. We are back to ground-level (i.e., bad) ozone again, the urban smog that we are desperately trying to eliminate. The term "nonattainment area" is EPA's regulatory-speak for counties that do not meet EPA clean-air standards. These counties have not "attained" clean air. An "attainment area," by contrast, is doing just fine.

In 2008, USEPA released a new list of ozone nonattainment areas. To the apparent horror of environmental groups everywhere, the number of counties with dirty air had grown significantly, from about 85 to 345. This statistic offered further proof, the environmental lobby cried, of how quickly the planet was dying. The press snapped the story up. In the absence of any other information, the environmentalist take on the situation seemed reasonable. However, this tale has more than one page. The actual reason that the number of ozone nonattainment areas grew was not that the air had gotten dirtier. It had not. In fact, the air quality in most of those ozone nonattainment areas had continued to improve, as it has for the past thirty years. Instead, it was the definition of "clean" that changed. Having made so much progress, EPA raised the bar by lowering the limits, calling on the nation's businesses and municipalities to reach a new and more difficult target.

In the beginning, the acceptable level of ozone was 120 parts per billion (ppb) or less, over any one-hour period. In 1997, the Agency revised that target down to 80 ppb, averaged over eight hours. Then, in 2008, the ozone standard was lowered again, to 75 ppb, averaged over an eight-hour period. The time period confuses the picture a bit, but each revision amounted to a more stringent standard. We know it is more stringent precisely because the levels of air pollutants that create ozone, volatile organic compounds (VOCs), and nitrogen oxides (NOx), have dropped more than 50 percent and 15 percent, respectively, over the last forty years. How could we emit less pollutants but end up with more pollution? Obviously, we cannot. The air is cleaner than ever, and the number of new ozone nonattainment areas does not mean we are polluting more. It means, simply, that our demands have increased.

This scenario is comparable to a high school changing the GPA requirement for graduation from 1.0 to 2.0. As a result, obviously, more kids fail to graduate. Let us also imagine that the average student's GPA in our mythical school rose at the same time the new graduation standard was established. In this circumstance, it would be disingenuous to focus solely on the fact that fewer seniors will not graduate, or to imply that the high school is doing a rotten job—that the kids are dumber than ever. Our hypothetical students are actually doing better, but the change in the GPA target means that graduations dropped at the same time. Implying otherwise would be to cherry-pick a convenient fact in order to bolster a sensational, but misleading, conclusion.

Cherry-picking is also an enormously effective way to manipulate a media that does not have the time, training, or inclination to do the sort of detailed, second-level analysis necessary to reveal the true picture. Environmental groups utilize the superficiality of most mainstream media analyses to their maximum advantage. In a similar fashion, these same groups use a subtle technique we might refer to as "fog generation." The opposite of cherry-picking, fog generation refers to the creation of an atmosphere so confusing that most people will eventually throw up their hands and tilt their opinion in the direction of the group they naively believe to be the least self-interested: the environmentalists.

Global warming (or "climate change"), today's most prominent environmental issue, is the classic example. According to environmental groups, every extreme climatic event—from hot spells to cold snaps, from tornadoes to hurricanes—proves their point. Scientists, they assure us, are in complete agreement on the issue. Computer models and mountains of weather station data "prove" their case. We are bombarded with data that supposedly demonstrates conclusively the hypothesis that Earth is rapidly turning into Dante's inferno. The weight of such "evidence" can seem overwhelming.

However, some of us have doubts. Portions of the ice caps and some glaciers may be melting, but they have been doing that for thousands of years. Some glaciers are growing. The heat waves, cold snaps, and average rise in temperatures are hardly unprecedented. Many argue that those events may be part of entirely natural cycles. The word "climate," after all, necessarily implies "change." Different models yield different results. Thousands of scientists without political agendas are more than skeptical about the global warming story. Their ranks continue to swell.

The mainstream media treat dissenters as though they were village idiots, quirky individuals liable to say anything and who are certainly not to be taken seriously. And why not? Even legitimate scientific journals such as *Chemical and Engineering News*—the signature publication of the American Chemical Society—fall into lockstep with conventional wisdom. As far back as 1997, in an editorial penned by managing editor Rudy Baum, *Chemical and Engineering News* officially dismissed any idea of a global warning debate. Baum claimed that the issue was too important to entertain any further discussion. That stunning declaration caused many scientists (including this author) to resign their memberships in the American Chemical Society. The essence of the scientific method, to which the American Chemical Society presumably still subscribes, is to encourage challenges to each and every hypothesis. Only by fending off each challenge can a theory become accepted as an established fact. However, a man such as Rudy Baum piously subverts the scientific method by declaring: "No, we do not give critics of global climate change the same amount of ink we give the far larger number of scientists who think global climate change is real. Quite bluntly, they don't deserve it." That statement is a remarkable, if sadly honest, reflection of the political nature of science today. Thus, even scientists are lost in the fog, abandoning the unbiased search for truth in favor of a political agenda. Can we possibly expect better of the mainstream media and the general public who have no scientific training?

In such an atmosphere, it is not hard to understand why environmental regulations have grown more and more oppressive. Though our world is actually cleaner than ever, most Americans are convinced it is dirtier. Of course, therefore, we need more rules. Furthermore, who should be the target of environmental regulation? Certainly not the individual. People do not believe that they personally contribute all that much to our seemingly grievous pollution problem. They are doing their part. They recycle. Their cars emit less gunk than ever. "Hey, it's not our problem," they will say. If the planet is dying—and it must be, because the trustworthy environmental lobby and its media allies tell us this is so—the disaster must be industry's fault. Those damned, dirty rotten polluters are killing us!

Generally, the EPA goes along with such logic, despite the fact that it knows that industry contributes only about one-half to one-fourth of the entire pollution picture—that includes solid, liquid, and air pollution. Industry has done its part, and then some, but it will always be asked to do more. Besides being a popular target, industry is also an easy target. When the EPA does the math, it is much simpler and more cost-effective to regulate 100 industrial sources emitting 5 tons apiece than it is to try to control 100,000 individuals emitting 0.005 tons each. However, this approach creates a problem. Industry has reduced its emissions so much that it is often practically impossible to find any more reductions. Yet the public demands further regulation. What to do?

Too often, the answer is more paperwork. Even if industry is following the right rules, it must do more to *prove* that it is doing the right thing. Industries have to keep more records, file more reports, and sign more certifications. When they make a mistake, which they inevitably will—given the complexity of the current system—the EPA will quickly intervene, demanding penalties. Every violation the EPA files is further proof that it is doing its job, satisfying the public's demand to restrain the nasty polluters. The fact that many of those violations have no practical effect on the state of an already healthy environment does not matter at all. Perception counts. Data does not.

This book focuses, therefore, on diminishing returns and counterproductive policies. In these chapters, we will examine different aspects of environmental regulation as well as the progress we have achieved. As we've made this progress, industry has paid the price. Frequently, the actions of bureaucrats have nothing to do with environmental protection. Sometimes, in fact, they are actually counterproductive.

Those of us who have been in the business for years have scores of stories that involve bureaucratic excess. We will tell a few of those stories, which are far from just anecdotal. They are, instead, symptomatic of a system that is out of control. Measured against the backdrop of all of our remarkable progress, these personal stories are especially maddening. In a world that is cleaner than ever, where we live longer than ever, why would we try to break the back of the employers who have done so much to provide our comfortable lifestyle?

There are no satisfactory answers to this particular question. The regulators have gone wild, and we have given them the power to do so. It is time to turn the tide.

CHAPTER TWO

GETTING THE LEAD OUT

LEAD WAS ONE OF SEVEN TOXIC COMPOUNDS INI-tially identified by the United States Environmental Protection Agency back in the 1970s. It was part of a list of Hazardous Air Pollutants that relatively few people would find reason to argue over, either then or now. The human body does not have much use for lead. At relatively low levels in the blood, it can do serious damage, particularly to children. Understandably, forty years ago Congress empowered the EPA to force the nation to eliminate lead from our environment as quickly as possible.

A number of regulatory measures helped accomplish that goal, vastly reducing the amount of lead that Americans have been exposed to since that time. The most important policy initiative leading to such success was the virtual elimination of lead in gasoline. Other efforts had significant effects as well. Today, it is the lead in old paint, on the walls of apartments and homes, that receives the most official attention.

Though the lead problem has been reduced to manageable proportions in this country, as opposed to considerably less healthy conditions in many other parts of the world, a number of folks in the United States are still interested in lead. From environmental groups to personal-injury lawyers, through—of course—the regulatory community, the directive to protect the public from lead is another cog in the machinery of the ever-growing risk-exploitation industry.

In the late 1990s, Fred Atkinson (not his real name) inadvertently found himself caught between the gears of an environmental crusade. An elderly gentleman of comfortable, but not extravagant, means, Atkinson ran afoul of relentless regulators for the crime of having purchased an investment property and unknowingly hiring the wrong company to take care of it for him. Like many senior citizens, Atkinson retired with a healthy, if not impervious, nest egg. It was enough to provide a start toward comfortable golden years, although not quite enough to ensure complete security itself. Hoping to find a way to make his money work for him, Atkinson eventually settled on one of the most resilient investments around, real estate. With some trepidation, he purchased a six-unit apartment building, in Chicago.

Part of his concern naturally revolved around managing his new investment. Maintaining the property, collecting rent, and finding good tenants involve much time and considerable expertise. Thus, like many small landlords, he hired a professional management company to look after his property. Let us call that company Blindside Management. In 1992, Congress passed the Residential Lead-Based Paint Hazard Reduction Act. This statute requires sellers and landlords of habitats built before 1978 to disclose the presence of known lead-based paint and its hazards. In that year, lead-based paint was banned in the United States.

It is important to emphasize use of the word "disclosure," for it summarizes the act nicely. Words such as "mitigation," "repair," or "removal" are not included in the act. No one has been forced to remove an ounce of lead paint because of this law. Action simply is not required by this law. Anyone who has bought a home built before 1978 has probably signed a lead disclosure statement—it is one of many forms in the imposing pile of paperwork that buyers must sign before they take legal possession of a property. As with most forms, chances are that one hardly notices it, or, chances are, one is not moved to do anything about it.

Because Atkinson's building was built before 1978, it was subject to the Residential Lead-Based Paint Hazard Reduction Act. However, he was not aware of the requirement. Why should he be? He had hired professionals to take care of business. Surely, they would do everything that was needed. Unfortunately, Blindside Management missed this requirement. Tenants did not receive the proper disclosure statements; eventually, the EPA and the Department of Housing and Urban Development (HUD) discovered the error.

Who is responsible for this oversight? Ultimately, from the government's point of view, it is the owner's responsibility. A sophisticated owner might ensure that his contract with a management company passed the liability along, but few inexperienced investors, such as Atkinson, are that savvy. The case was ultimately referred to the Illinois attorney general's office for prosecution, which translates to the pursuit of penalty dollars. Sometimes penalty demands are proportionate to the crime. Other times, which occur too often, the government practically extorts money far out of proportion to the severity of the alleged crime.

Much of the punitive fury depends on the government attorney assigned to a particular case. If the attorney is a crusader or is ambitious—or worse, both—weaker opponents get hit the hardest. Big settlements are great for a young assistant attorney general's career. Those successes secure headlines that attract the attention of superiors. Two practical approaches insure a big settlement: find a transparently irresponsible big corporation, or find someone without the resources to fight back. Fred Atkinson fell into the latter category.

The initial penalty demand from the attorney general was a shade over $140,000, a spectacular amount for the size of the case. To get a sense of scale, consider the way that the EPA and HUD settled a lead disclosure case with Apartment Investment and Management Company (AIMCO) in 2002. AIMCO's settlement covered more than 130,000 apartment units in forty-two states. The amount of their penalty was a mere $129,580. That works out to about $1,000 per unit, as compared with more than $23,000 per unit that Illinois demanded from Atkinson.

This case is all the more amazing when one considers that Atkinson's units did not present an actual hazard. His was a well-maintained building, not a slum full of crumbling paint chips. Nor would Atkinson have to remove any old paint. His buildings did not contain any lead-based paint at all. He—or rather his agent—had only failed to have the right pieces of paper signed.

The regulatory process is supposed to ensure equity, but sometimes the process itself is the penalty. With little choice, Atkinson hired a skilled environmental attorney from a nationally known law firm to argue his case. That kind of expertise does not come cheap. As his attorney began to assemble the evidence needed to protect him, Atkinson quickly found himself racking up bills at the rate of $350 per hour. Regardless of the final decision, he was already a loser.

State regulators would eventually knock the penalty down to a little less than $25,000, but it would take a great deal of time and money before that happened. The assistant attorney general in the case was surprisingly intransigent. Although Atkinson's attorney produced reams of evidence showing that the penalty was inappropriate, the assistant attorney general seemed determined to make a stinging example of an old man and his retirement plans. It was only by going over her head—and thus earning her undying enmity—that Atkinson's lawyer would knock the punishment down to something at least moving in the direction of reasonable.

Atkinson's story raises questions that suggest a continuing theme: Who should be held responsible when a rule is broken, and should degrees of punishment be proportional to degrees of intent, let alone the degrees of actual or probable harm? Some regulators, and certainly those involved in the decision-making process in this case, place intent far down the list. What matters is money. Whoever has the most—be it a giant corporation or a modest investor—pays a hefty price.

That cost might be proportional to other factors, such as the degree of risk, the magnitude of the problem, whether the mistake occurred through negligence or through knowing and willful disregard of laws and regulations, and, perhaps most important, how effective the penalty will be at discouraging similar transgressions in the future. Of these factors, many would argue that the last should carry the most weight. What is done, Shakespeare pointed out, is done. Regulators should use the guilty to encourage innocence in the future. To their credit, that is, in fact, the stated intention of most environmental agencies.

Yet, in cases like this, the state often seems simply out to extort an extra pound of flesh. Should the government, one has to wonder, be able to sue for punitive damages? Those who support aggressive enforcement of lead rules, even in cases where there is no actual lead to be found, argue that a strict program of negative regulatory reinforcement is a necessary evil. Lead is such a severe and pervasive human health risk, they claim, that the government is obligated to use every regulatory weapon at hand.

The public, reinforced by messages in the media and a climate of fear decades old, is largely sympathetic to that logic. How sound is the basis for this policy? In the twenty-first century, does lead pollution in the United States present so terrible a health risk that people in Fred Atkinson's situation deserve to have their retirement income put at risk when they have caused no tangible harm?

As noted, lead and humans do not mix very well. Children are particularly susceptible. The National Academy of Sciences associates high lead levels in kids with a variety of neurological and behavioral disorders in children. At high levels in the bloodstream, lead causes brain and kidney damage, and, in large enough quantities, even death. It can be an extremely effective poison. What levels, however, are dangerous? "Dangerous" is, and ought to be, a relative term. From a scientific point of view, the only way to judge relative points of view is to delve into the complex, confusing, and often frustrating realm of the mathematician: numbers. Do not be afraid. Numbers are surely evil things, but they can be tamed. It is all a matter of sorting them out.

In 1996, EPA Administrator Carol Browner trumpeted an environmental triumph: after twenty-five years of work, the lead threat was defused. "The elimination of lead from gasoline is one of the great environmental achievements of all time," Browner said in a 1996 press release. "Thousands of tons of lead have been removed from the air, and blood levels of lead in our children are down 70 percent. That means millions of children will be spared the painful consequences of lead poisoning, such as permanent nerve damage, anemia, or mental retardation."

Her statement sounds pretty encouraging. Perhaps, but money is still to be made from lead, and plenty of personal-injury lawyers do not want any part of this whole "progress" theory. Consider the following dissertation from Ed Herman, an attorney with the law firm of Brown and Chauppen. Under the heading "A Lead Paint Lawyer's Story," Herman wrote:

> Exposure to lead can lead to a life time [sic] of serious medical problems. Children who maintain high levels of lead can suffer brain damage, learning disabilities, speech problems, hyperactivity, loss of learning capacity and attention deficit disorder. It's been estimated that lead poisoning may be a factor in 76,000 cases of mental retardation each year. There is no question that lead poisoning is directly responsible for an alarming number of American children never being able to achieve their full potential.

We can be sure this was penned by personal-injury attorney because Herman manages to say absolutely nothing while sounding terribly authoritative and concerned. What is a "high blood level?" We are not going to find out here, but clearly, it must be a chronic problem. Just look at that long list of woes that "can" be caused by these "high" levels. Lead "may" even be a factor in 76,000 cases of mental retardation per year. So might cosmic rays. Maybe evil aliens from the planet Zoltron are responsible. Who knows?

Furthermore, the problem is so severe that an "alarming number" of American children may not achieve their full potential. What exactly does "alarming" mean? What is the magnitude of the actual number meant to alarm the public? Probably the most alarming thing for Ed Herman would be if he did not manage to cash in on his fair share of those 76,000 cases of potentially lead-induced mental retardation.

According to the Centers for Disease Control (CDC), the level of lead in the blood of an average American has decreased remarkably over the past thirty years. In 1976, the average person had 14.9 micrograms of lead per deciliter of blood (a unit abbreviated as mg/dl). What does that mean? Any level above 10 mg/dl is considered unhealthy today. Got it? Almost thirty years ago, we typically had 14.9 mg/dl, which is bad, compared to the officially good 10 mg/dl *safe* level.

Measured another way, more than 88 percent of Americans had blood levels above the magic 10 mg/dl level back then. That is decidedly *bad*. By the year 2000, the average American had a mere 2.2 mg/dl of lead in his or her blood. Only 2.2 percent of the population topped the 10 mg/dl standard. The number of American children with lead in their blood above the level of 10 had dropped as well, from about 13.5 million in 1976 to less than half a million in 2000—a decrease of more than 95 percent.

Clearly, the elimination of lead in gas made the dramatic numbers possible. In 1973, more than 200,000 tons of lead were pumped into the air each year, by way of the internal combustion engine. By 1996, leaded gasoline sales were limited to a small number of users, including some airplanes, racing cars, farm equipment, and marine engines. Lead emissions from gas dropped 99 percent, from over 200,000 tons per year to less than 2,000. As lead poisoning diminished in importance in the United States, some environmental advocates and risk minimizers turned their attention, in a more appropriate direction, to the globe as a whole.

According to the World Health Organization, between 15 and 18 million children in developing countries suffer permanent brain damage because of lead poisoning. While the average blood level of lead concentration dipped to 2.2 mg/dl in the United States, it could be ten to twenty times that level in developing countries, according to the World Bank. Levels in Mexico City, for example, approached 25 mg/dl in the 1990s, while levels in Bangkok, Thailand, reached 40 mg/dl. The continued use of lead in common products such as cosmetics and the failure to ban leaded gasoline are the biggest culprits in these cases.

Clearly, lead is a much bigger problem in many other parts of the world than it is in the United States. However, the fact that other people have worse problems does not necessarily mean that America's issues are insignificant. Lawyers like Ed Herman, counting up his 76,000 potential lawsuits, would surely argue that lead remains a very big deal indeed.

Thus, crusading newspapers, such as the *Milwaukee Journal Sentinel*, would claim that "thousands of Milwaukee children are being poisoned each year. The poison is lead in old paint." That accusation is pretty spectacular. If we accepted Herman's claim of a doomed 76,000, then Milwaukee alone would house about 3 percent of them, even though the city hosts less than 0.5 percent of the total U.S. population.

Such conflicting claims among lead alarmists might lead to a couple of obvious conclusions:

1. Keep your family out of Milwaukee, unless
2. you are a personal-injury attorney who specializes in lead poisoning.

Perhaps, instead, it is time to take an even closer look at those damned numbers. So far, we can safely state a few facts about lead in America today:

- There is far less lead in our bloodstream than there was thirty years ago.
- Sources of lead ingestion, chiefly represented by leaded gasoline, have dropped dramatically over the same period.
- Whatever the magnitude of the problem today, in terms of lead contamination, it is much better now, and it is a lot cleaner in America than in many countries.

Let us take a closer look at that official level of 10 mg/dl of lead in blood. What does it really mean? It is important to note, first, that the Centers for Disease Control and Prevention did not lower the alarm bar to 10 mg/dl until 1991. Before that, it was 25 mg/dl. The CDC's action represents a continuing theme in the environmental industry. After a goal has been achieved, the standards are lowered. This action both ensures that an appropriate level of alarm is maintained among the press and public and serves to guarantee continued employment for the lobbyists, lawyers, and regulators who depend on a climate of fear to make a living.

The American Academy of Pediatrics recommends treatment for lead poisoning when the concentration of lead in blood exceeds 45 mg/dl. Remedial measures, such as removing lead paint from walls, are recommended when blood levels top 25 mg/dl. How, therefore, did we get to 10 mg/dl? To a large extent, we can find the reasons in a 1979 study by Dr. Herbert Needleman, then with the University of Pittsburgh. Needleman's work suggested that 10 mg/dl was the appropriate benchmark, and he pointed to behavioral and learning problems in inner city kids as the "evidence" for his claims.

Both the University of Pittsburgh and the *New England Journal of Medicine*, which published his research, would later backtrack from that work, which many fellow scientists found flawed. Inevitably, the public finds such disagreements among scientists equal parts dull and unsolvable. If they cannot understand the details of the issue themselves, many members of the public tend to believe the scientist who offers the scariest scenario. The rationale is that if one prepares for the absolute worst case, one is sure to be safe in all cases.

Needleman's strongest argument was that inner city children lived in older buildings and were, therefore, more likely to be exposed to lead paint. As a result, he maintained, they exhibited less academic achievement. Needleman's logic was terribly flawed, because other factors could easily explain punitive consequences. Inner city children are also much more likely to be poor, and poor kids do worse in school—for a variety of reasons.

In the broadest sense, could one possibly tie the trend in lead exposure to academic statistics? As lead exposure has dropped precipitously, test scores among our children have declined.

If today's lead levels are such a big factor in brain function, should not the test scores have gone up—or at least held steady—as the amount of lead in our children's blood declined so spectacularly? Clearly, other factors are much more important.

However, a microscopic, and therefore often distorted, analysis sets the tone for modern environmental policy. True, lead exposure can be a health hazard. However, the degree to which that risk is significant in this country is too easily skewed by the shrill rhetoric of the self-interested and by the powerful inertia that every public health and environmental measure seems to generate. For people such as Fred Atkinson, who do not even come close to the dirty-rotten polluter profile that Hollywood and the media have popularized, the results can be disastrous.

Their sin is ignorance, not callousness. By now, environmental concerns have been addressed so well for so long, and the likely effects of a misstep (such as Atkinson's) are so minimal, that it's impossible not to wonder if sober risk analysis long ago gave way to irrational demands born of fear.

CHAPTER THREE

LUSTING AFTER DOLLARS

IN A FIELD FULL OF ACRONYMS, THE SHORTHAND for EPA's Leaking Underground Storage Tank program is arguably the most enjoyable: LUST. The program addressed a very real problem, but it went far beyond what was needed and ended up wasting billions of dollars.

It also confused many ordinary people who ran into expensive, hidden minefields. Lifelong investments in property were rendered worthless overnight. Almost nobody understood why. Take these observations from a New England man who watched a neighboring property lie vacant for over a decade for reasons he couldn't fathom. "The soil-contamination thing can all be a matter of timing," Connecticut businessman Cam Bortz wrote.

When I first moved into this area, I looked at a former gas station that was for sale—cheap. It had three bays, another large room off the side, and best of all, two 2-bedroom apartments on the second floor, everything I could have ever wanted for a home-based shop.

The problem on this property was the ground around the gas tanks. The tanks had been pulled in the late eighties, and the EPA determined there were 15 cubic yards of "contaminated" earth. The cost wasn't in removing the earth; it was that this dirt was considered "toxic waste" and would have to be transported to an EPA-approved site in South Carolina, at a cost of two to three million dollars. What struck me is that the EPA apparently didn't think this dirt was dangerous enough to make anyone move it until the property was sold.

In 1998 the property finally sold, and it was renovated into retail space. The soil? Well, it seems that the dirt is only considered "contaminated" for ten years after the tanks are removed. The ten years were up in '99, and the property suddenly soared in value and was promptly purchased and renovated. Not a shovelful of formerly "contaminated" dirt was ever moved. What this proves (to me, anyway) is that the EPA is just like any other pack of paper-pushing nitwits. They can f*** up someone's whole life one day, and a day later have no jurisdiction or further concern with a site. Let me tell you, I feel so much better knowing how diligently they protect me. Yeah. Right.

Bortz's down-home observations were spot on. For years, the EPA ran a hideously expensive program that spent billions of dollars to relocate—not remove—waste, without doing much in the way of environmental good. USEPA would eventually fix most of the excesses, but not before thousands of service-station operators had been driven out of business by the cost of huge, cleanup programs that went far beyond what was necessary to protect human health and the environment. To understand what happened and why, we have to go back to the 1980s, when LUST regulations were in the developmental stage. Most everyone recognized that leaking tanks were a problem.

A large number of underground tanks were installed in the 1940s and 1950s at service stations as automobile sales boomed. The typical life expectancy of these bare steel tanks was about thirty to fifty years. So, by the time we hit the 1990s, a great many tanks would be expected to fail due to corrosion. If they are destined to fail anyway, why bury the tanks underground at all? There are a couple of reasons: efficiency and safety.

An underground tank leaves the ground above accessible for other uses. In the case of service stations, which are often located on relatively small parcels of land, space is often a big issue. Locating a tank underground also ensures that any liquid or fumes that might escape from the tank will be absorbed by the surrounding earth, rather than collecting in potentially flammable or explosive concentrations above ground. There is a lot to be said for underground engineering in terms of safety, but leaks did cause environmental headaches. The biggest danger from leaking tanks is groundwater contamination. About half of all Americans get their drinking water from groundwater. Even a small gasoline leak could contaminate large quantities of groundwater. A 10-gallon gasoline leak, for example, contains enough benzene to render over 10 million gallons of groundwater unfit for human consumption.

However, when groundwater is not used for drinking water, leakage is not nearly as big a concern. Mother Nature is pretty effective at cleaning up man's mistakes, given sufficient time. Contrary to what most environmental groups would like us to believe, she is not a frail, doddering grandmother. Mother Nature is a tough old broad, and it is very hard to get the best of her. When groundwater is not an issue, leaking tanks are not much of a worry. Naturally occurring microbes in the soil will literally consume the contaminants. A few years after a leaking tank is removed, the surrounding soil will be as pristine as it was before the tank arrived.

Given these two very different levels of risks—depending on whether groundwater was at risk—many engineers advocated a system of graduated cleanup objectives when LUST regulations were first developed. If groundwater contamination could affect drinking-water supplies, a more stringent set of standards, they said, should apply. In cases where groundwater was not affected, or where groundwater was not used for drinking water, why set the bar unreasonably high? Why not let Mother Nature take care of the problem?

The difference in the two approaches shows up in the bottom line. The biggest expense in many tank removals is not the cost of pulling the tank out of the ground; it is the price of getting rid of contaminated dirt. A typical tank pull may cost $20,000 to $50,000, but when soil removal and disposal are added, the bottom line can climb to hundreds of thousands, and sometimes millions, of dollars. Why tack the expense of massive soil removal onto projects in situations where the soil did not matter and would clean itself up anyway?

Later, after they finally admitted that dissenters were correct, USEPA officials would blame the agency's failure to apply reason in the first place on "the need to start-corrective action programs quickly." Apparently, according to EPA logic, the only way to do something quickly is to do it stupidly. The LUST program effectively begin in 1988 when owners of underground tanks were notified that they had to upgrade, replace, or close their underground tanks by December 22 of that year. New tanks would be held to tough new standards, designed to ensure that they would not leak. If they did, the leaks would be detected and contained.

Replacement was the preferred option of many of the sites affected. In the first six years of the program, over 200,000 LUST owners either cleaned up their site or were in the process of doing so. With very few exceptions, regulators insisted on the removal of every grain of contaminated soils, whether drinking water was involved or not. The cost of replacing tanks soon exceeded the resources available to pay for the remediation.

In theory, government would help pay for the cleanup. The federal LUST Trust Fund, financed by a penny per-gallon gas tax, is a minor contributor, providing about $70 million per year for remediation. States provide the bulk of the funding, at a rate of about $1 billion per year, most of which is raised through additional gasoline taxes. Unfortunately, the combined $1.1 billion could not cover all the expense that private operators were facing. A disturbing trend developed: overwhelmed with impossible expenses, the people who owned underground tanks would walk away from their property instead of cleaning it.

The system needed fixing. However, because the EPA was not concerned about putting independent service-station operators out of business for no good reason, the feds were finally motivated to act. As an agency official laconically put it in a 1995 memo, "[W]hen reimbursement is not immediately available, corrective actions tend to slow down." Translation: "Since we are paying for it and we need to show results, maybe it is time to factor reason into the equation." The resulting directive, Use of Risk-Based Decision-Making in UST Corrective Action Program, is generically known as "Brownfields" in the business. Distilled down to its essentials, the directive reversed the policy of the previous six years. Instead of doing everything they *could* do, underground-tank owners would now have to do only what they reasonably *should* do.

Each cleanup site would be judged individually, based on its unique merits and risks. If groundwater was used for drinking water, or a school was nearby, or some other high-risk factor was involved, the site would have to be restored to pristine conditions. If drinking water came from another source and there were no public uses nearby, more reasonable objectives would apply. It made sense, as the dissenting private-sector engineers back in the 1980s knew it would. However, the Brownfields policy was, by any measure, an example of what environmental groups would normally disdain: "backsliding." How could USEPA relax an environmental regulation without subjecting itself to howls of protest from the outraged

Environmental Defense Fund and the Sierra Club? The answer to that question reveals the true political nature of these organizations and all similar beasts.

Brownfields became a reality in 1995, when a Democratic administration was in power. Because Democrats can do no wrong as far as environmental groups are concerned (as opposed to Republicans, who can do no right), Brownfields was universally hailed as a triumph of environmental efficiency. It was an especially odd conclusion, as many of the same groups had rejected the very same concepts in the 1980s, but that was while Republicans were in charge.

Even with Brownfields in place, there are plenty of unscrupulous operators in the private sector lurking about to sabotage and pillage the unsuspecting entrepreneur. Certainly government has no obligation to fix all the problems of the private sector, but such cases serve to further illustrate how environmentalism has grown into a business with all the ethics of personal-injury law.

Before commercial or industrial sites change hands today, an Environmental Site Assessment—commonly called a "Phase I"—is required by the lenders who finance the transaction. Phase 1 projects are detailed investigations into the history and use of the land involved. They are conducted in order to ensure that the owner is not inheriting any expensive environmental problems.

Let us say that a possible issue is identified, such as underground storage tanks that were removed twenty years ago. What if those tanks leaked and residential contamination remains? In such cases, site owners will usually authorize a Phase 2 assessment, in which the consultant drills into the ground to take soil samples for analysis. Both Phase 1 and 2 programs are relatively inexpensive, at least compared with what often follows. When contamination is found, it has to be addressed. If that translates into a cleanup, the costs can give Donald Trump ulcers.

Unscrupulous consultants run a three-part sting operation that goes something like this:

1. "Of course we can do a Phase I for you, Sir. As a matter of fact, we can do it cheaper than anyone else."
2. "That Phase I revealed a couple of possible problems. Don't worry—they're just possible. We'll have to do a little drilling to see what's there."
3. "You're not gonna believe this, but we found something. Actually, we found a lot of something. EPA is going to make us clean it up, and—yeah—I know it's crazy and I know it's expensive, but what can we do? EPA said so."

The process does not always work that way. Plenty of ethical environmental consultants look out for their client's interests and do more than is actually required. They will take advantage of Brownfields programs to avoid or minimize a cleanup. They will look after a client's money as though it was their own. But the system clears the way for people without much in the way of a conscience to make easy money. The EPA will always bust you if you are not doing enough, but they will never let you know if you do too much.

It would be different if business owners believed they could trust the EPA. A neutral agency could act as a check to the charlatans, as government agencies do in many other parts of our lives. However, when the environment is the issue, bureaucrats cannot afford to be neutral—not really. A savvy business owner will seek out a number of opinions in the private sector and use the free market to beat the huckster. A more trusting, more naive, and more pressed entrepreneur is that much more likely to hand over a fortune to the person he believes will protect him. A little more agency discretion could solve the problem in a great many cases, but we should not expect that to happen any time soon.

CHAPTER FOUR

MORE TOXINS, PLEASE

REGULATIONS ARE NEVER AS FRUSTRATING AS when they are counterproductive. The rules have their own rigid logic, and the people who enforce those rules are bound to that logic, regardless of actual effects. Most regulators take shelter in the type of strict interpretation that would make a hardcore fundamentalist of any religion proud. With a few blessed exceptions, the regulatory world is staffed with people who cannot, or do not care to, succeed in the performance-driven private sector. They do not worry about bad results. In fact, they do not think about results at all. Their focus is entirely on the process and ensuring that they can always say that the road to the final decision is 100 percent defensible. Where that path may lead, is not their problem. In this "green" era—with Barack Obama's EPA tightening emissions standards so much that most people in industry believe they will be unable to comply without completely shutting down their processes—the lessons of the past can teach us a lot about what we can expect in the future.

Abbott Labs in North Chicago, Illinois, was the scene for a classic case of regulatory means circumventing any sensible ends. USEPA presented the pharmaceutical manufacturer with an odd choice: continue cleaner operations in violation of a rule, or follow the rules and increase emissions. It was a classic illustration of a continuing theme: environmental regulations often are not about the environment; they are about the paperwork. Abbott's case goes back to 1997, when USEPA introduced new rules designed to reduce emissions of toxic air emissions, also known as "hazardous air pollutants," or HAPs. In the Agency's inventory, as we shall see, are many such rules. This particular set is known as the "Boiler and Industrial Furnace" regulations (BIF).

The goal of the BIF regulations was admirable: to ensure that hazardous waste burned for fuel, in industrial boilers and kilns, was properly destroyed. BIF established standards designed to prove that this method of destruction did not inadvertently result in the release of too many HAPs into the atmosphere. A part of the program was a requirement to conduct emissions tests. Any unit that burned HAPs would have to compare what was actually emitted to emissions allowed under the rule.

At the time, Abbott operated a coal boiler, which it used to generate power and raise steam, both of which it used in quantity. The company supplemented its coal use with some waste solvent that was injected into the boiler. As hazardous wastes go, the waste solvent was not very hazardous and, in fact, was much more chemically similar to gasoline than any noxious material. The solvents were not especially toxic or contaminated. However, having been used in the pharmaceutical manufacturing process—and having come into contact with chemicals that are classified as HAPs—they were considered HAPs themselves. Innocuous as the waste stream might be, the fact that Abbott used it for fuel meant that the boiler was subject to BIF.

Abbott conducted the required emissions tests. The results might have been encouraging. They clearly showed that the solvents had been destroyed even more efficiently than the rule demanded. Yet there was a problem: emissions of certain heavy metals exceeded BIF standards. But here is the rub: BIF standards for heavy-metal emissions were more stringent than heavy-metal emission standards for boilers burning coal alone. As a matter of fact, a coal-only boiler would not have been subject to a heavy-metal standard at all at the time.

Clearly, therefore, any heavy metals emitted from the boiler did not come from the waste solvent—the solvent did not contain heavy metals. The only possible source of the offending emissions was the coal itself. If the agency insisted that Abbott stop burning solvent in order to conform with BIF, the company would have to burn more coal to make up the difference. Burning more coal could only increase the amount of heavy metals that the plant emitted. Yet, for USEPA, the choice was simple. Abbott could cease and desist its practice of burning waste solvent and come into compliance, or the company could continue operations and be cited for violations of the BIF rule. Would following the former course have a negative effect on the environment? Sure. That was a regrettable, but ultimately immaterial, consequence. The rule was all that mattered.

That Hobson's choice might have been avoided had this been a matter of state jurisdiction. Some states have appeal structures by which a company can ask for a second look at an agency decision. If the appellate board agrees that the environmental or economic costs are not worth the cost of strict interpretation, it will grant some sort of relief from the rule—most often in the form of a variance (of limited term) or an adjusted standard (long term). Abbott's dilemma was custom-made for that kind of second look. Unfortunately, at the federal level, there are no appeals beyond the court system, and judges are very reluctant to rule against USEPA when technical matters are an issue. In practice, the courts are not much of an appeal mechanism at all.

In a case like Abbott's, the court would consider a narrowly defined set of issues. Did Congress properly delegate authority to USEPA to apply the rule properly and fairly? (Yes.) Did Abbott violate the terms of that rule? (Yes, but—.) The court cares no more about the extenuating circumstance (the "but") than the Agency does. From a company's point of view, there are no options. Compliance meant not burning solvent, so Abbott stopped burning it. Instead, it started shipping its waste solvent to an approved, off-site incinerator. There, the chemicals would be destroyed as completely as they had been on-site at Abbott. However, the trucks transporting the waste would now add their own pollutants to the atmosphere; Abbott would be forced to buy more coal (becoming less energy-efficient) and, most important, the company's increased coal usage would put more heavy metals into the atmosphere.

Did USEPA's fundamentalist stance make any reasonable sense? Obviously not. But we might ask another question: How did the agency arrive at such a hard-core position in the first place? To figure that one out, we will have to step back to 1970 and the birth of the Clean Air Act. In the beginning, the Agency was directed to look at air pollution in two ways: in terms of criteria pollutants and hazardous air pollutants. Criteria pollutants were, and are, the pollutants emitted in largest quantity; thus, they presented the most immediate threat to human health and environmental welfare. These are nitrogen dioxide (NO_2), sulfur dioxide (SO_2), ozone (O_3), carbon monoxide (CO), particulate matter (PM), and lead (Pb). Congress directed the agency to implement specific control measures to reduce emissions of all of these problem pollutants.

At the same time, Congress recognized that other air pollutants might be emitted in far smaller quantities but could still pose local threats to health and welfare. The universe of everything else was designated hazardous air pollutants. EPA's charter, as far as these HAPs were concerned, was clear: the agency was directed to set standards for toxic air pollutants individually, based on the particular health risk of each. Using this risk-based formula, the EPA regulated seven HAPs between 1970 and 1990: asbestos, benzene, beryllium, inorganic arsenic, mercury, radio nuclides, and vinyl chloride. These standards cut toxic air emissions by 125,000 tons per year, or by about 2 percent.

That percentage impressed environmental groups very little. EPA was not doing its job, they cried. The fact that the Agency was only able to identify actual risk in two cases was immaterial. USEPA said that the risk-based approach was "difficult and minimally effective at reducing emissions." The term "minimally effective" is the key. Perhaps the risk-based approach was minimally effective at reducing HAP emissions, but was it really minimally effective at protecting public health?

When something labeled "toxic" passes under the public eye, emotion, rather than science, is usually the most important factor. Toxicity is a matter of dose, as sober scientists have observed since ancient times. A particular compound may kill you if you drink it, but a few parts per billion of the same compound can have no effect at all. If we do not accept that dose matters—if we say that nothing greater than absolute zero is acceptable—we then create an unsolvable problem. Entirely natural processes create "toxic" chemicals at small concentrations. One can, for example, find toxic air pollutants in the parts-per-billion level in human breath. Why should a few parts per billion of a *toxin* such as toluene be of more concern to us because it is emitted from a smokestack instead of a mouth?

A wholly risk-based approach would seem to address that issue. When man-made toxins create risks that significantly exceed the natural baseline, regulators can step in. Otherwise, why bother? When Congress readdressed the problem of air toxins in 1990 with the passage of the Clean Air Act Amendments, legislators hit upon a new formula. Instead of considering what we should do, legislators decided to expand their vision to what we *could* do.

New, technology-based standards were the answer. Congress created another acronym, MACT, which stands for Maximum Achievable Control Technology. It directed USEPA to look at what was being done to control HAP emissions in 178 source categories, or types of manufacturing processes. The Agency was then directed to develop a specific set of standards based on the best that was being done by the companies engaged in the same business within each source category.

Let us say that you run a plastics company, for example. Following the 1990 statute, USEPA was supposed to develop emissions standards for you to follow based on what the best of your competitors were doing.

Having decided that risk did not matter, Congress not only said that technology was all that counted, they focused the technology discussion on industrial sources. Given that industry is supposed to be responsible for all the environmental ills of the universe, that should not be surprising. Is it a fair conclusion? According to USEPA data, industry accounts for about one-fourth of all HAP emissions. Mobile sources, which include cars, trucks, tractors, airplanes, and other things that move, create about 50 percent of air toxins. The balance comes from what are called "area sources." Area sources are everything else, from man-made consumer products, such as nail polish and hair spray, to natural sources, such as volcanoes and forest fires. The latter is a surprisingly large source of HAP emissions.

When we consider the toxic pollutants of greatest concern, the picture becomes even more surreal. USEPA has identified thirty-three particular HAPs, dubbed "urban toxics," of special concern. These are the toxic pollutants most commonly emitted in urban areas and, therefore, the ones to which the majority of the population that lives in urban areas is likely to be exposed. Industry accounts for less than 10 percent of urban toxic emissions, according to EPA data. Think about that. For the majority of us living in the United States, the biggest air-pollution toxic risk we face (whatever that means) is not created by the big, bad factories; rather, it is a result of the vehicles we drive and the products we use.

If we distill that down further, we will find that about two-thirds of urban toxic emissions can be accounted for by two specific chemicals: benzene and formaldehyde. The former is largely emitted by vehicles that use gasoline, and the latter is created by anything that burns fuel: engines, boilers, hot-water heaters, and gas furnaces. Industry's role in producing these toxins is, by any measure, fairly insignificant. No matter. It is cheaper, and far more popular, to crack down on factories. No doubt that approach will be effective. MACT regulations were designed to cut HAP emissions by 1.5 million tons per year. That is about 25 percent of all toxic air emissions (6 million tons) identified by USEPA in 1990.

That reduction will cut toxic emissions from industry about as much as they can be cut. Through a combination of reformulations, process changes, and improved control technologies, American manufacturers have set the world standard for hazardous-pollutant-free operations. Nevertheless, certain industrial sectors will still fall under intense public and media scrutiny. Medical-waste incinerators, for example, are a popular target of the fear industry, despite the fact that the few ounces of toxic emissions emitted by the average medical waste incinerator is merely baseline noise compared with the millions of tons spewed from tailpipes. Still, there are not many emissions reductions left to reduce in the majority of cases. One cannot tap a dry well. So what happens next? Three EPA initiatives will take center stage in the years to come: mercury regulations, an analysis of "residual risk," and mobile-source reductions.

Amusingly, USEPA frequently refers to mercury emissions as "man-made." Man does not create mercury, of course. Outside of a purpose-built atom-smasher, this author is not aware of any means by which man could create the element. Man does not produce mercury, we relocate it. The big concern is that coal-fired power plants are relocating too much mercury from coal deposits (where it is a naturally occurring trace element) to waterways, where fish and other wildlife can retain it. The amount retained is also trace, but it is enough to alarm some public-health advocates and, by extension, make the EPA nervous.

Accordingly, USEPA hopes to cut the amount of mercury emitted by coal-fired power plants—which accounts for about half of all man-made mercury emissions nationwide—from "almost zero" to "really close to zero." Many scientists who conduct risk analysis have concluded that the entire issue is much ado about less than nothing, but no matter. New mercury risks are inevitable. The only question is how much will they cost.

Moreover, there is strong evidence that most of the airborne mercury in the United States is not generated in this country. In order to justify mercury controls in the United States, environmental advocates will often quote United Nations Environmental Programme (UNEP) reports that identify China, India, and the United States as the three largest mercury emitters on the planet. This is true, but a closer look at mercury-emissions data puts America's role in clearer perspective. The following data is taken from UNEP's latest mercury-emissions inventory, published in 2008, which summarizes mercury emissions as of 2005:

SOURCE	2005 MERCURY EMISSIONS (TONS)	2005 MERCURY EMISSION (PERCENT OF WORLD TOTAL)
China	695.5	42.6
India	177.2	10.9
United States	129.7	7.9
World Total	1,631.5	100.0

USEPA estimates that about one-third of all mercury emissions generated within the borders of the United States are deposited within the country. When compared to background mercury, from both natural sources of mercury deposition and other global sources of man-made mercury emissions (chiefly China), little is to be gained from a practical standpoint by further reducing mercury emissions from power plants in the United States. Yet, requirements to do so move forward, and the Obama administration has proposed the most draconian cuts in mercury emissions from power plants ever considered, reductions that will be enormously expensive to realize, if, indeed, the goals can be met at all.

The hysteria over the supposed dangers associated with mercury emissions is a microcosm of a larger theme: if environmentalists and the EPA can find substantive risks, they will redefine the terms themselves. This idea was built into the Clean Air Act Amendments of 1990, and we are still dealing with the consequence of this approach today. Having required industry to do all it can, the next legally required step is for USEPA to consider which industries should do some more. Residual-risk analysis, required under the Clean Air Act Amendments of 1990, direct the agency to go back to the old formula: examine industrial emissions and determine if the public is in any danger.

The public was not at risk in 1970, so one might conclude that the results of such an analysis should be obvious. However, risk in 1970 does not have much to do with risk as defined in the twenty-first century. The Agency has clamped down hard on selected, unpopular industrial sectors and will continue to do so, especially under the current administration. Aside from the need to satisfy the public and media by applying more pressure on evil factory owners, there is the issue of job security. A lot of people are employed in the business of environmental regulation. They need something to do.

Finally, there are those mobile-source emissions—the largest single generator of air toxins. USEPA recognizes that, of course, and has proposed and implemented a variety of rules designed to clean up what comes out of tailpipes. Benzene emissions were reduced by 40 percent between 1993 and 1998, and the agency predicts that data will show that an overall reduction in vehicle-based toxic emissions of 1 million tons per year was achieved by the end of 2010, as compared to 1996 levels.

Add all of those rules together and one can calculate a remarkable achievement. Between 1990 and 2010, toxic emissions will have been cut by more than half. Apparently, there was little reason to believe that those emissions were very dangerous in the first place. We have every reason to pat ourselves on the back. Whether or not we do will depend entirely on the administration in power. If it is a Democratic administration—a supposedly pro-environment regime—the massive reductions will take center stage. If a Republican occupies the Oval Office, the environmental groups founded by the opposition will focus on whatever remains. If those groups are prone to point with horror at a few dozen tons of mercury when the GOP is in power, they will have no problem declaring that two or three million tons of *toxic* emissions are a sure sign of Armageddon. Millions of anything sell newspapers, even when all those zeros actually mean nothing.

Notwithstanding the massive reductions in toxic air emissions that were realized during the Bush years, Barack Obama's EPA is determined to slash the little that remains dramatically—costs be damned. For example, in 2010 the EPA proposed new regulations to address the small amount of HAPs emitted by industrial boilers. The standards proposed represent something unprecedented in the history of environmental regulation. In the past, creating a new emission standard involved a bit of haggling: the EPA proposed something, environmental groups wanted more, and industry said they could not afford it. In the end, the final regulation was a compromise that satisfied nobody and everybody. Industry had to shell out a few more bucks, but environmental groups could crow that—because of their efforts—emissions were being reduced.

The academic types who permeate the Obama administration have tossed that process aside. In the case of industrial boilers, the standards proposed are so ridiculous that industry is not even bothering to grumble. The numbers are unachievable, and everyone outside of the beltway knows it. Even state regulators know it. As one old hand at a state regulatory agency told me, "USEPA is happy to let you operate a factory these days, so long as your emissions are zero." In their headlong rush to go green, the policymakers in power have lost any sense of perspective and any ability to soberly weigh risks versus rewards.

Thousands of companies like Abbott Labs could surely testify to that truth, were it not for the fact that American industry has been cowed by the environmental lobby. They will do almost anything to avoid being the latest victim of the next Erin Brokovich. That might mean paying millions to install controls that accomplish nothing, and that might mean accepting rulings that require them to emit more than they otherwise would. It does not matter. When toxins or any other kind of pollutant are an issue, American manufacturers know they cannot win as long as they continue to operate a plant in the United States of America.

CHAPTER FIVE

JOBS vs. RETRIBUTION: THE PRICE OF PUNISHMENT

DOMINIC IMBURGIA AND PHYLLIS MUCCIANTI ARE part of a typically American success story. In 1975, they were young, ambitious businesspeople, making money in the packaging industry, selling plastic bags to companies that needed attractive, convenient ways to package their products. They were earning a good living, but they realized they could make more if they managed the business themselves. Why make somebody else rich? They understood the process. They knew the market. They had drive and boundless energy. They decided that is was time to make a bold move.

Bold moves are not made frivolously, as any entrepreneur can attest. Both Imburgia and Muccianti had families that were counting on them. They could not ignore the risks. As they like to recall, the pair sat down at a kitchen table, hashed their plan out, and decided to take a chance. They chose an odd name for the new company, Packaging Personified, Inc. However, for anyone who knows the partners, it was not that odd a choice at all. It was a reflection of the way Imburgia and Muccianti like to do business: developing relationships, relying on character, and adding a personal touch to everything they do. Customers and employees became part of the family, as likely to discuss golf, travel, or grandchildren over lunch as they are to talk business.

In time, Packaging Personified would grow into a smooth-running, profitable company with over 100 employees, millions in sales, and scores of large corporate customers in the food, consumer-products, and pharmaceutical industries. Imburgia and Muccianti built their own plant outside Chicago, producing the plastic, cutting the bags, and printing on them according to their customers' specifications. In the midst of that growth, they failed to notice that they had grown large enough to fall under Illinois EPA environmental regulations. As is usually the case, theirs was an innocent mistake. Most people assume that environmental rules were designed for U.S. Steel and General Motors, not for small businesspeople who start their company across a kitchen table.

Unfortunately, this is not the case. The scope of environmental rules reaches deep into the heart of small businesses. Ignorance of the law, as we have all been taught, is not an excuse. Imburgia and Muccianti believed that they were being environmentally responsible. They employed technologies to cut down on pollution, both in their choice of equipment and in the kind of inks they used. When Illinois EPA inspected their facility, twenty-five years after the company had been formed, Imburgia and Muccianti were understandably shocked to find that they had been branded bad guys. Worse news was on the way, when they learned just how bad they were deemed to be.

Given their type of operation and levels of emissions, Imburgia and Muccianti's plant, according to Illinois rules, should have an incinerator (called a "thermal-oxidizer" in modern enviro-speak) to destroy emissions from the process. The company dutifully complied, spending over a third of a million dollars to collect emissions from its printing presses and destroy them in a thermal oxidizer. Lawyers, consultants, tests, and additional energy costs would add over $200,000 more to the bill.

Imburgia and Muccianti grumbled, as would any businessman forced to pay unproductive expenses, but they paid. Fair was fair. If these were the rules, then they had to follow them.

Meanwhile, more business opportunities appeared. The recession that followed 9/11 served to cull out some of the weaker players in the packaging business. Overseas competition—unhindered by excessive environmental, labor, and liability expenses—forced profit margins down. The least efficient American companies folded, leaving an opportunity for people like Imburgia and Muccianti, who emphasized productivity and who understood the value of personal attention and quality.

They purchased a rival packaging company in the state of Michigan, quickly transforming it from a cash sinkhole into a profitable, job-generating, thriving concern. The future looked bright, and the team looked even further outward, hoping to apply their winning formula in more locations across the nation. It was then that Illinois EPA's penalty demand arrived in the mail. The cost of the company's mistakes? More than $800,000. To say that the partners were shocked is to vastly understate their reaction.

They were appalled because they had always tried to do the right thing. They had used the best technologies they could find, and, when they found they had to do more, they spent over half a million dollars to get into compliance. Now the EPA wanted them to write a check for almost a million dollars? It was inconceivable— even more so because they knew that their competitors in the region had not had to pay even a tenth that much for the same type of mistakes. The difference, such as it was, involved timing and awareness.

Imburgia and Muccianti's competition had approached the Illinois EPA in the mid-nineties, when the EPA was designing new rules that would apply to plastic packaging companies. Those competitors argued—successfully—that incinerators would be too expensive for them to build and operate and would not make a significant difference in air quality in the Chicago metropolitan area in any case. These companies were granted relief, fined nominal amounts, and were not required to install controls. Packaging Personified, unaware of the changes in store, was not part of this privileged group.

Air quality in the Chicago area continued to improve. By the end of 2005, smog levels had decreased so much that Packaging Personified's emissions were no longer deemed a threat to the environment. The air was getting cleaner, and the role of small businesses in the pollution picture was, consequently, much less important. That did not matter in the inflexible regulatory view. It was ironic. Science fiction writers throughout the years have speculated that man would turn over too much authority to the inflexible logic of machines. In fact, mankind has surrendered its discretion to the inflexible logic of the printed word. The Illinois EPA decided that the letter of their regulations demanded an $800,000 penalty, and *that*, by God, is what the state would receive. Mitigating circumstances simply do not—cannot—matter in the regulator's world.

Whatever discretion the Illinois EPA might have otherwise exercised was eliminated by the Illinois administration and its seemingly insatiable need for cash. Governor Rod Blagojevich was running up billions in debt, creating new entitlement programs that Illinois could not afford. The governor proceeded to squeeze every last dollar out of business and industry to close the gap, increasing taxes and fees on business by over $2 billion—a staggering amount for companies in the Prairie State. Bigger environmental permitting fees and tougher penalties were part of the formula, too. Before Governor Blagojevich, a small company like Packaging Personified might have been able to negotiate a reasonable penalty. With the governor desperate for every dollar he could get, evenhanded negotiation was no longer an option. That left Imburgia and Muccianti in a difficult position. They were Illinois natives. They had begun, built, and nurtured a company for more than three decades in their home state. Their employees were part of their family. But $800,000? How could they justify such a number?

Could they pay such a price? Technically, the answer was probably yes. The partners had profited from the fruits of their three decades of labor. They had personal wealth. However, the Illinois EPA was presenting them with a cruel choice: surrender a large portion of what you have worked so hard, and so long, to achieve, or go away. To be sure, "go away" was an option, a choice that many beleaguered Illinois employers have taken over the last few years. Imburgia and Muccianti had established a thriving operation in Michigan. Other states were offering tax breaks and financial incentives. To leave all they had built in Illinois would be hard, but—in their eyes—the state was not leaving them much choice.

The partners approached the dreadful decision slowly. They moved more and more of their production capacity to the friendly confines across Lake Michigan. They looked at opportunities in the Carolinas. They began to evaluate the price of fighting back, like suing the Illinois EPA for making demands that would force their company to move out of state.

In terms of actual emissions to the environment, the company is in full compliance with Illinois rules, as it has been since Packaging Personified installed controls in 2003. In the years since their errors were discovered, air quality in the Chicago area has continued to improve. In spite of these facts, a huge penalty continues to hover over the company's head, almost a decade after Imburgia and Muccianti identified and corrected their error. A company like Packaging Personified can barely withstand a penalty so egregious, but even if it manages somehow to avoid that penalty, the process itself is penalty enough. To date, the partners have spent close to half a million dollars defending themselves against the charges.

The Illinois EPA, like most regulatory agencies, says that such large penalties are necessary, even in the case of a small business like Packaging Personified, for two reasons: (1) such penalties discourage other companies from making the same mistake, and (2) it is necessary to "level the playing field" by ensuring that some companies do not make extra profits by skirting the rules and thus getting a leg up on their compliant competitors. Admittedly, behind these sorts of justifications is a certain logic, but it is the sort of logic that often breaks down under close scrutiny.

The deterrent effect on small businesses comes into play the moment the violation notice hits the door. It is a frightening event, for most small-business owners believe that the EPA has almost unlimited police powers over their affairs. One of the first questions they almost always ask is, "Will the EPA shut me down?" That rarely, if ever, happens unless lives have been directly put at risk, but such is the perceived power of the agency. Like the majority of small businesses caught up in an EPA enforcement action, Packaging Personified's first response was to seek help from experts in the field, including me. The marching orders we were given were simple: do whatever it takes to bring the company into compliance, the cost be damned. The nightmare of dealing with inflexible bureaucrats and the time and expense associated with mounting a defense are immensely painful, not only in terms of finances. The seemingly endless saga takes an emotional toll on the people involved. The thought that a state or federal agency might take away all that a business owner has worked so hard to build makes for many a sleepless night.

It is hard to argue that the competitive playing field should not be level, but many times the USEPA and state agencies use dynamite, supposedly to even out the ground of the marketplace, when a gentle grade adjustment is all that is necessary. Federal guidelines dictate how regulators are supposed to calculate the economic benefit associated with noncompliance. These methods are meant to take the human factor out of the equation and ensure the unbiased, consistent calculation of economic benefit. However, one can never remove the human factor from any calculation or any model. The results of such computations are only as good as the information fed into them; that information necessarily involves human beings making decisions. Since, on the regulatory side, the people making such decisions generally have little or no understanding of the intricacies of the business sectors they are passing judgment on, those decisions are often deeply flawed.

Such was the case when the Illinois EPA calculated Packaging Personified's economic benefit for noncompliance. At best, a sober review of the facts showed that the company had earned an extra $75,000 during the period that it was not properly controlling emissions. Arguably, Packaging Personified did not make an extra dime during that period. Yet, somehow, the Illinois EPA managed to come up with an astronomical figure that was more than ten times higher than any reasonable calculation. Worse, once the agency decided on such a number, it was stubbornly unwilling to back off even a dollar, no matter how much evidence contradicted their faulty assumptions. This kind of regulatory intransigence and bureaucratic bungling is the pattern time and time again, in state after state across the nation. The effects on the business climate and on the economy have not, to my knowledge, been calculated, but in my mind there is no doubt that this toxic environment poisons business decisions every day.

The end of Packaging Personified's particular story is yet to be written, but unless the Illinois EPA can see the wisdom of backing down—at least somewhat—from its stubborn stance, it seems likely that this remarkable company will abandon its roots and settle in a place where its mistakes will not exact such a steep a price. When and if that happens, we should ask ourselves, Who was the winner? By any sober analysis, it would be hard to say that the people of Illinois, or the state's environment, will have gained anything at all.

CHAPTER SIX

RESTORATION MEETS FRUSTRATION

T HEY USED TO BE CALLED SWAMPS STAGNANT, mosquito-infested backwaters that farmers could not drain fast enough and builders could not fill quickly enough. Eliminating swampland was once a point of American pride as little as thirty years ago, another symbol of our ability to wrestle progress from nature's obstacles. Conservationists began to rethink the murky issue in the late twentieth century. Swamps would be reborn as wetlands, now identified as home to diverse, important species of plant and animal life and a vital cog in the natural machinery that maintains the health of our waterways.

It was the first President Bush who initiated the "no net loss of wetlands" policy in 1990, in response to the new science. Environmental groups, hardly predisposed to praise any Republican administration, applauded the move along with their more mainstream conservationist cousins.

Two decades after it was launched, the initiative remains in place, passing from the stewardship of President Clinton, through that of its founder's son into the arms of the current administration. Administered by the Army Corps of Engineers, the Federal Wetlands Protection Program has demonstrated an unbroken track record of success, despite the claim put forth by more than one interest group that George W. Bush's presidency was an environmental disaster.

Yet, as thousands of new wetland acres are created across the nation each year, administrative issues linger. If the nation hopes to enjoy an economic revival in the future, those problems must be addressed. During the long building boom that we enjoyed before the economy collapsed, billions of dollars in development projects were funneled through a wetlands-approval structure not nearly large enough to manage the flow. Nature was being protected, and improved, but at a cost that affected everyone. It should be a lot easier to act responsibly.

Why protect wetlands? Simply put, they are filters. Wetlands handle silt deposits that, if they made their way to a stream, can throw a wrench into the mechanics of waterway life.

Wetlands are also better equipped to process other contaminants, too. When properly balanced, the combination of slow-moving water, unique biochemistry, and special forms of plant life act as a mini treatment plant. Indeed, more and more civil engineers and city planners use wetlands as a part of their overall water-treatment program. "We realized they can be an asset and a tool to build better communities," said Sharon Caddigan, legislative chair for the Illinois chapter of the American Planning Association. "Wetlands areas can be used to manage stormwater and give the towns the opportunity to create greenways as well, for example."

There are other reasons, of course. Concepts like biodiversity and resource management sound merely theoretical to the everyday ear, but conservationists and environmentalists would agree that they have concrete value.

Responsibility for wetlands management falls on the Army Corps of Engineers, which administers the Clean Water Act 404 Program. It requires developers first to look at the property where they wish to build and determine if any wetlands are present. That determination is not as simple as it seems (I'll write more about that later). If inspectors find wetlands, a three-step chain of regulatory logic kicks in.

Step one is avoidance. The Corps works with the developer to find a way to leave the wetland as it is. Perhaps there is an alternate building plan that will serve both man and nature, for example.

Step two is minimization. Perhaps not all of the wetland has to be drained or filled. The Corps looks for means to keep the acreage affected as small as possible. Historically, about 20 percent of the permitted projects that might have had an impact on a wetland are able to avoid doing so in the end, in full or in part.

That brings us to step three, the step that is most commonly implemented. If there is no way to avoid the wetlands, or if a developer can avoid only a portion, the no-net-loss-of-wetlands policy demands that whatever is taken must be replaced, at least in kind, and often in abundance. "Mitigation" is the term of art. It is the option employed in about 80 percent of 404 permits, leading to an actual increase in wetland areas across the nation.

We have more than met the goal of avoiding a net loss of wetlands established by the first President Bush, but there is a catch: the actual amount of wetland areas in the country as a whole has decreased.

That national decrease can be attributed to a single state: Louisiana, where the bayous on the coast are disappearing into the sea. Coastal drilling for oil and natural gas and a host of other factors—including natural wave and wind action—are to blame, pulling away some shoreline foundations. That issue is unique, however, and should not stain the overall success of the 404 program.

When we take Louisiana out of the equation, the picture becomes clear. In a typical year, mitigation efforts result in a net gain of wetlands from permitted development projects, ranging from 130 percent to 200 percent of the original area. That is a heartening statistic that many environmental groups nonetheless choose to ignore, focusing their attention instead on projects cherry-picked to play up controversy. The history of overall progress is largely ignored.

Consider this all-too-typical case in point. "The Bush administration's proposal to restore (more) wetlands is a contradiction," Ed Hopkins, of the Sierra Club, said while the younger Bush was president. He delivered his remarks at the site of a particular development and restoration project that drew his group's ire. "While we still need to see the details, it seems clear that we'd be better off if the Bush administration simply enforced the law that's on the books." At the time, President Bush had announced a program to accelerate wetland recovery, the step that prompted Hopkins skeptical remarks. Even without further refinements, it is hard to understand why anyone would consider the Bush administration's wetlands program a failure.

In 2003, for example, 21,000 acres of regulated wetlands were developed, only to be replaced by 43,000 new acres. The Bush administration's first four years in office saw a net gain of about 21,000 acres per year of wetlands, compared to about 19,000 per year during the eight Clinton years. (The National Fish and Wildlife Service, the agency tasked with tracking wetlands, has not yet released data later than 2004).

Contrary to common thinking, wetlands are not always wet. They do not even have to be damp. They're defined by a complex set of scientific criteria, the most important of which involve the type of soil, the hydrology of the land (a factor that considers its wetness), and the species of plant life present. By that definition, acres of land that look high and dry to the untrained eye fall under the 404 program. There is even a class of property, "farmed wetlands," that qualifies, even though it may not meet any of the official criteria. Farmed wetlands are swamps that were drained or filled for agricultural use in the past and turned into fields. Before those areas are used for any other purpose—to build a housing development, for example—they must be returned to their historical state, or at least an equivalent amount of new wetlands must be created elsewhere.

Wetlands also vary in quality, from ponds ringed by common cattails to exotic fens full of rare species. When a developer fills a wetland, the Corps sometimes judges the quality using a point system. Whatever is replaced must be of at least equal, and more often greater, total value. The formula considers both quality and quantity. Thus, creation outstrips destruction each year. The Supreme Court theoretically limited the Army Corps' jurisdiction over wetlands in its 2001 SWANCC (Solid Waste Agency of North Cook County) decision, but the practical effects of this ruling have not been as awful as many environmentalists predicted.

The SWANCC case was a landmark in the environmental community. It divided wetlands into two regulatory categories: those under federal control and those that are not. The decision traces its roots back to the nineties, when SWANCC filed plans to build a balefill (second cousin to a landfill) in the northwest Chicago suburbs. The Corps opposed the project on the basis of a wetland on the site. In this instance, the wetland was clearly isolated. That is, it did not connect to any other waterway system that, in turn, crossed state lines. Therefore, the federal government had no interest in the project, SWANCC argued. When the case eventually made its way to Washington, the Supreme Court agreed. Henceforth, there would be two types of wetlands: those connected to interstate waterways and thus under federal control, and those that stand on their own and are strictly a matter of local interest.

Regulators, environmentalists, and developers still wrestle with that decision, trying to figure out which is which. It is not always plain to see whether or not "waters of the United States" are affected. Clearly, a wetland that lies adjacent to and drains into the Ohio River still falls under federal—that is, Army Corps—control. That is easy. But how about a set of tire tracks that leads to a ditch, which empties into a creek that leads to a stream, which feeds a small river that ultimately runs into a major river? Could those tire tracks be a federally protected wetland? The water drained and the value gained by our theoretical tire ruts are ridiculously tiny, but some would argue that the Corps has both the right and the duty to protect them, or that such "wetlands" are "jurisdictional," to use the proper term of art.

On the other end of the spectrum, some substantial but isolated wetlands lie in land depressions that cannot possibly drain into federal waters. According to the SWANCC decision, those areas are a matter of local interest only. Some environmentalists say that developers have used the SWANCC decision to fill isolated wetlands at an alarming rate. In the absence of any other factors, that might be true. But the facts are (1) the Corps is far from the only sheriff patrolling swamps, and (2) the broad interpretation of "waters of the United States" leaves a lot more area in Corps control than alarmists would have one believe.

In many regions of the country that have wetlands, state, county, or local municipalities have regulations that are even more restrictive than the federal version. Sometimes all three are involved. In these areas, even the most isolated wetlands are every bit as protected as those the Corps monitor. In other places, aggressive Corps enforcement will prevent all but the most hard-headed of developers from filling any wetland without due caution. Are there cases when the Corps in less active and there is a vacuum of local regulation? Surely there are. Does that mean that some wetlands are filled and not replaced? Undoubtedly.

However, given an aggressive environmental community and a media generally sympathetic to their causes, it is hard to believe that the few isolated wetlands that are filled each year—and not replaced— are enough to give Mother Nature much heartburn. The acres gained under the 404 program tell the more significant and encouraging story. These facts bring us to the ultimate problem, one which does not involve environmental quality, but program efficiency and economic growth. If there is a reasonable complaint about the 404 program, it comes from the developers who have to wrestle with a system that is not nearly large enough to handle the work they hope to do.

Never famous for patience in the first place, developers find the delays imposed by the 404 program especially frustrating. In many cases, this permit is the last step before a project can go forward, arriving well after every other bit of paperwork has been ready for months. More often than not, developers direct their frustration toward the Corps. "By and large, it's not that builders and developers object to getting permits or taking care of their responsibilities," said Chandler C. Morse, wetlands policy analyst for the National Association of Home Builders. "Instead, it's that the Corps has nearly limitless power to regulate however they want, which often translates into wide discrepancies between how different Corps districts assert their jurisdiction and field staff's ability to drag the permitting process out for as long as they want. Builders and developers often have no idea what will be regulated or any idea how long it will take to get a wetlands permit, a process that can stretch into years. Home builders, in order to successfully perform their business, need a consistent and predictable regulatory program."

Caught between the environmentalists, who would only be satisfied if no 404 permits were ever issued, and developers, who need their permits the day before yesterday, the Corps knows it cannot please everyone. However, many of those involved agree that the process needs to move more quickly. "There are about $200 billion worth of private construction projects that have to funnel through just 1,200 Corps regulators each year," said George Dunlop, who was a principal deputy assistant secretary of the Army, in the Office of the Assistant Secretary for Civil Works in the Bush administration. "It is not unusual for people to have to wait six months to a year, or longer, to work their way through the permit process. The delay and uncertainty impose an enormous burden on property owners that not everyone appreciates, and it can have a negative impact on the economy as a whole."

More resources to process more permits more quickly is the answer, according to Dunlop. With two decades of environmental success to look back on, it is hard to argue that the 404 program has not earned the kind of trust that justifies such improvements. Yet any proposals to streamline the system inevitably run afoul of the environmental lobby. Indeed, the Obama administration is certain that we need a more restrictive wetland-permitting process, not a smoother, faster mechanism. History shows that most environmental groups will tag any attempt to increase regulatory efficiency with the label "backsliding," even if there is no actual effect on the environment. There is even less evidence than usual to believe "blacksliding" is an issue in the case of wetlands. "The objective isn't to consume wetlands," Chandler Morse concluded, reflecting the mind-set of most builders these days. "It's simply to speed up a process developers have accepted as part of their business."

Clearly, the issue is not about doing the right thing. There are no longer any valid arguments about that. The value of wetlands is well established. Wetland program goals have been, and continue to be, exceeded. The challenge is to find a way to do the right thing more efficiently. Meanwhile, developers and the Army Corps of Engineers continue to wrestle with 404, hoping that it will eventually get a little easier to protect our natural resources while creating wealth and supporting badly needed economic growth at the same time.

CHAPTER SEVEN

PAYING FOR SOMEBODY ELSE'S MISTAKE

BACK IN THE EARLY NINETIES, A FIRE VIRTUALLY destroyed a building housing Group Eight Technology, Inc., a Michigan company engaged in the scrap and recycling business. In the aftermath of the blaze, the company and its carrier, Wausau Insurance, began to deal with the sticky problem of cleaning up the mess. A portion of that cleanup involved six electrical transformers, which can be environmental fire bombs. Older transformers often contain polychlorinated biphenyls (PCBs), a type of oil that is a special target of environmental regulations, most notably the Toxic Substances Control Act (TSCA). Should PCBs be found in a transformer, they require extra special handling and disposal. Thus, Wausau made sure that the transformer oil was duly tested. The results were good: no PCBs were found in any of the six. A contractor was hired to remove the oil and dispose of it.

The contractor did his job, but he threw in a bonus. After pumping out the six transformers he had been hired to clean, he noticed a seventh. Figuring that he was doing the company a favor, he emptied that one as well and proceeded to dispose of the contents at a nearby landfill.

Unfortunately, that seventh transformer was filled with PCBs. About 70 percent of the oil consisted of that offensive chemical. Inevitably, the landfill would later become a Superfund site, not only because of the PCBs but owing to other hazardous materials as well. USEPA declared that it was a Superfund site under the Comprehensive Environmental Response, Compensation, and Liability Act (CERCLA).

USEPA decided that contamination at the landfill was an "imminent and substantial endangerment." Those are four very weighty words under CERCLA. They are almost a sorcerer's spell. Invoke them and the EPA can make magical, even miraculous, events occur. All it takes is money, and the great thing is this: the money is never the government's. Once the agency invokes those words, it can make the earth move—literally. They can circumvent judicial review. They can reach down and pluck millions out of the deepest pockets they find, no matter how small a role the well-heeled party may have played in creating the "emergency."

As far as Wausau was concerned, it was hard to see what was either imminent or substantial about the oil that their client's contractor had inadvertently dumped in a landfill. The landfill, also located in Michigan, was frozen solid in the middle of one of the coldest Midwest winters in history. In order to remove the PCBs from the site, cleanup crews would first have to use propane heaters to melt the frozen oil. No matter. The EPA declared that the contamination would be removed within twenty-four hours. And so it was, at a cost of $3.5 million. Had the project waited, as it should have, until more temperate spring weather, the price would have been a couple hundred thousand less. Wausau protested, but it did as it was told.

It wasn't enough.

USEPA wanted more. They demanded that Wausau pay to clean up all of the PCBs on-site, not just their own. This directive invoked another CERCLA four-word magic spell: "joint and several liability." The theory in this case is not completely without merit. At the average hazardous waste site, it is impossible to separate the mishmash of garbage. Determining who put what where, or which particular bit of contamination caused the most problems, is not possible. In the absence of such evidence, CERCLA provides for a simple formula: whether you contributed to a fraction of the problem or to a majority of it, you are responsible for all of the cleanup costs—potentially anyway. A typical CERCLA Superfund cleanup consists of a dizzying number of prescribed steps, but the most important ones to any company subject to the statute are (1) identifying the companies who contributed waste to the site, (2) figuring out which are still in business and actually have assets, and (3) a battle among all parties to determine who will pay what.

When a big, well-heeled company is involved, it is like hitting a jackpot in Vegas. An Exxon-Mobil or Wausau Insurance is the ideal PRP (potentially responsible party), whether it contributed one drop of contamination or 10 million gallons. Environmental attorneys flock to CERCLA cases like buzzards following a cattle drive through Death Valley. A lot of money is to be made off of CERCLA, and one does not have to be an especially good attorney to cash in. It's more a matter of managing negotiations between the government and other PRPs. Even better, the fees that attorneys charge for those negotiations are lost among the millions of dollars in cleanup costs that their clients ultimately have to pay. For many an incompetent lawyer, a big CERCLA case is like winning the lottery.

Consequently, "joint and several liability" was a terrific hit. For the EPA, it represents an easy way to pay for the maximum number of cleanup projects. For the attorneys representing the companies who pay for those cleanups, it is a seemingly endless source of cash. Who is the loser? Obviously, the companies who shell out the cash— and justice itself. No matter how well considered, there is something inherently wrong about a big corporation shelling out millions to clean up a site where some mid-level manager may have mistakenly sent a single drum of goo.

Wausau appeared to possess the counterspell to "joint and several liability." Chemicals, like people, have DNA-like signatures. Wausau determined the chemical signature of their client's PCBs. They could precisely identify which oils were their responsibility and which oils they had nothing to do with. That should matter, right?

It didn't matter. USEPA told Wausau that it had to clean up all the PCBs on-site, whether or not the chemicals came from Wausau. The insurance carrier swallowed hard but ultimately complied. It was not worth the argument. Yet EPA wanted more. The agency could not let such a fat checkbook go away without grabbing every penny available. It had "joint and several liability" to fall back on, so it did not have to worry. "While you are at it, clean up all of the Total Petroleum Hydrocarbons on-site, too," the agency said. Total Petroleum Hydrocarbons is a big chemical category, representing any type of organic chemicals—solvents, fuel oil, gasoline, and others—the vast majority of which have nothing to do with PCBs. The agency also directed Wausau to clean up any sulfuric acid present at the dump. This included drums of virgin sulfuric acid that could have been resold on the commercial market for good use, instead of being transferred to another disposal site.

At this point, Wausau had enough. They sent a clear message to USEPA: "You made us clean up our own PCBs, even though they did not pose any danger to anyone. You made us clean up PCBs that we had nothing to do with. Now you are asking us to clean up chemicals that could have come from Mars and could not possibly have anything to do with our client. You're insane. Enough is enough. This stops here."

This decision would prove to be critical. Wausau made a tough choice, moving from official cooperation into the ranks of those who refused to comply with an order from USEPA. The fact that it had done what was asked up to this point did not matter. Once one says no in any part of the process one is officially an obstructionist in the eyes of the regulators. That type of behavior usually brings serious repercussions, and it did in this case. Wausau would go to court after the fact, in an effort to recoup some or all of the $3.5 million the company had been bullied into spending. The company would be rebuffed, chiefly because it had been officially declared "noncooperative" by USEPA.

To a large extent, the science did not matter. Trained in the law, not science, judges grow as weary of technical arguments as does the average journalist or citizen. When judges have to choose between a paid shill arguing for the evil industrial sector and a paid shill arguing for the EPA, they inevitably opt for the latter. "The courts refuse to get involved in the science," Wausau's attorney, Bill Anaya would later observe. "To reverse the agency, the court has to determine that the EPA was both arbitrary *and* capricious. If they're only arbitrary or only capricious, it doesn't matter. As long as they go through the process, they'll win."

CERCLA thus translates to a standard in which industry is guilty until proven innocent. Even worse, business does not have an opportunity to prove its innocence until well after the fact, and only then within a forum that is officially predisposed to discount any defense that a private-sector operator might offer. The inherent inequity extends even further in the case of large corporations. The larger the company, the deeper the pockets, the more unfair the process is likely to be.

Site investigations are one of the first steps in any cleanup project. These studies involve drilling holes (usually a lot of holes), taking samples, and analyzing those samples to determine exactly how far the contamination extends. The cost of a site investigation can vary wildly, depending on the site and the nature of the contaminants. However, site conditions are not the biggest cost driver. The regulator in charge has much more power over the purse in this step than in most any other program. Consider the contrast with LUST.

Under the LUST program, the owner performing the cleanup comes up with an investigation plan, which the government then must approve. Because the money to pay for the cleanup comes out of public funds, there is a built-in incentive to approve investigation plans that are cost-effective while still being responsible. The regulator has final say, but a natural check in the system encourages reasonableness because the regulators are spending at least a portion of their own money. It is not that way with CERCLA. The EPA does not mind demanding a Rolls-Royce when a Chevy will do, as all the money used to foot the bill comes from the private sector. Further, once the government has identified a handful of those precious PRPs, there's not a lot of incentive to find others who should contribute a fair share. "USEPA hasn't done enough to enforce against nonparticipating PRPs," veteran CERCLA attorney Susan Franzetti observed. "Part of the round of stepping up to the plate should be that the EPA should join with the PRPs to put pressure on the non-cooperative PRPs."

So what has CERCLA accomplished over its thirty-year life? It has been a massive engineering accomplishment, keeping excavation equipment moving to and fro throughout the nation.

Under CERCLA, over 10 million cubic yards have been moved, over 1.5 billion gallons of hazardous liquids removed from sites, and over 250 million gallons of polluted water treated.

Response actions fall into two categories, short- and long-term. Short-term removals, under which the Wausau case fell, involve cases where the agency has determined there is imminent and substantial endangerment. Long-term cleanups present no immediate threat but are large enough to involve enough potentially dangerous materials to require action. Long-term projects are established by the National Priorities List (NPL). The entire process is long and arduous and, as noted, designed in such a way that the legal arguments are typically protracted and expensive. According to USEPA data, the average cleanup cost per CERCLA site is over $25 million. With over 1,200 sites, either closed or ongoing, that is more than $31 billion in cleanup costs, and the vast majority of that total is paid for by private means.

By any measure, CERCLA has been a massive effort. Clearly, though, it is a process that needs fixing. Of all the programs,

CERCLA is arguably the bulkiest, and needlessly so. Under the Bush Administration, USEPA proposed scores of reforms to CERCLA, designed to make cleanup quicker, less costly, and more efficient. For the companies involved in the process, and especially the big ones who pay the bulk of the bills, it was a long-overdue step. Predictably, environmental groups disagreed. They twisted all attempts to simplify a process into attempts to destroy it. With little or no knowledge of the unnecessary pain involved, it is easy to see how the public might easily swallow the environmental industry's spin. The Natural Resources Defense Council (NRDC), for example, screamed that CERCLA reform would "exempt the military from virtually all responsibility for toxic munitions contamination on its 25 million acres of operational ranges."

Why do environmental groups complain about CERCLA reform efforts? Because CERCLA reform would restrict the definition of contamination to occurrences that cross range boundaries. That is a subtle issue, one that can ensnare not only the Department of Defense but the local gun club as well. The ground of a shooting range is filled with lead slugs. Of course it is. That is pretty much the point of a shooting range, is it not? Yet lead is a hazardous substance. So when do lead slugs go from being discarded ammunition to constituting an environmental threat? The answer, perversely, depends on whether you choose to move them.

The law provides that a substance cannot be classified as a hazardous waste if it is used for its intended purpose. When a slug is fired and falls to the ground, that is part of its intended purpose. However, the moment one tries to clean it up, an important line is crossed. Moving the expended slug is not an "intended purpose." By touching it, one can create a "waste" and, by extension, a potential Superfund site. DOD ranges are full of such "waste in waiting" and will continue to be, as long as the military uses them to enhance military readiness. As written, CERCLA could allow the long arm of the EPA to reach into those sites to remove lead, depleted uranium, unexpended munitions, and the other flotsam and jetsam of military training.

And what is the point? A range is not a residential development. Military ranges are isolated for a reason: to keep the public protected from the activities confined therein. By proposing to exempt the interior of ranges from CERCLA, the EPA took a reasonable and logical step. They asked only for the military to keep their activities within military sites, and they agreed to apply the full force of a powerful law when mistakes crossed the borders. It was a sensible move, one that would have done nothing to endanger the health and welfare of the public or the thoughtful protection of our natural resources. No one proposed firing depleted uranium slugs into sequoias. All the Bush administration's EPA wanted to do was to recognize an existing land use and to acknowledge that what happens within that land is of little environmental consequence to the rest of the nation.

This DOD issue is but one example of reforms that made sense but still managed to incur the wrath of the environmental industry. These CERCLA reforms aimed to make the process simpler, quicker and less costly, not to reduce the criteria that determine when a cleanup is necessary and what the remedial actions will be.

The environmental industry does not understand, or perhaps does not care about, what CERCLA reform is meant to do. For environmentalists, "reform" equates to "backsliding," and why not? Every time the process becomes more efficient, the industry loses some of its influence. If one can quietly clean up a Superfund site in six months instead of ten years, there is not much opportunity to go before the media and wring hands about the process. As time goes on, there will be fewer and fewer Superfund sites. We are already seeing the trend, as attorneys who prospered during CERCLA's boom years have nearly been reduced to selling apples on the street. Even though they represent industry, the last thing they want is reform. They want more cleanups, more lengthy negotiations, and—most important—more fees. Unfortunately for them, companies have gotten a lot smarter about how they dispose of the hazardous wastes and how they manage potential for accidents. As sophistication in industry has grown, the number of Superfund sites has steadily declined.

For the environmental industry, that was further proof that the Bush administration gave industry a free pass. The green brigade expects that manufacturers will remain terminally stupid until the end of time. On the contrary, smart business decisions have led to the success and the very programs environmentalists champion. Superfund sites have declined in numbers not because USEPA became more lenient, but because the sheer cost of the cleanups has made industry more careful. Increasingly, big companies do the right thing. Not necessarily because they are good citizens—although many of them are—but simply because it is too damned expensive not to be.

CERCLA will live on. It is too important not to. The only question is, In what form? If reformers have their way, it will continue to be the nation's first line of defense against potentially catastrophic releases and contaminated disposal sites, but the process will become much more equitable for all. Should the environmental industry continue to be successful in its efforts to quash reform, CERCLA will continue to be what it has long been: a horrendously expensive statute that makes a mockery of the proposition that one is innocent until proven guilty.

CHAPTER EIGHT

POWER PLAYS

IF ONE COMPARES A GRAPH OF ECONOMIC GROWTH with a graph of power usage, one will notice the inevitable correlation. As the economy grows, so does energy use. The environmental industry hates that comparison. Because it is sure we are terribly inefficient, it constantly protests that we must make better use of our resources. The fact that we generate more revenue for our energy, and then promptly redistribute a substantial fraction of those dollars to worthy public causes in this country and around the world, is of little consequence to the environmentalists. They measure efficiency strictly on a per-person basis, not in terms of products, services, and good deeds. By the latter, more telling measure, America is quite efficient, indeed.

Still, today's culture of environmental hysteria has created a strange ambivalence among many average citizens. They want more power to run their computers, fuel their SUVs, and air-condition their 3,500-square-foot homes. However, they do not want to deal with the need to produce that energy. In the environmental industry's unique fantasyland, we would meet our increasing energy needs with renewable sources. Windmills, solar arrays, and electric cars will solve every problem. It is a fine, high-sounding idea, but it has little to do with reality. As the late governor of Washington Dixie Lee Ray pointed out, it is all a matter of packing power into a reasonably sized, inexpensive package.

A wind farm will take up several dozen acres of land to generate perhaps 50 megawatts of power. As a sidelight, all of those spinning blades will execute a few hundred, or maybe a few thousand, birds along the way, but that is yet another issue. The same goes for solar power. Even if solar cells were 100 percent efficient, and of course they are anything but, it would take hundreds of acres to generate the power needed to run a medium-sized town. The inefficiency is reflected, as it should be, in the expenses. It costs a penny or two to generate a kilowatt of electricity at a nuclear plant. Burning coal or gas costs about triple that. When we get to wind and sun, the price can double, treble, and sometimes quadruple beyond the cost of fossil fuels.

Electric cars are a great concept. When driven, they do not produce any pollution. However, there is an environmental price. The electricity that goes into the batteries has to come from somewhere. More often than not, that electricity is generated by burning fossil fuels. Given the inherent inefficiency of sending electricity across miles of power lines, electric cars do not end up being much of an environmental benefit.

Yet panaceas such as wind power, solar power, and "pollution-free" electric cars are more popular than ever. Such dreams capture the imagination of the public, which longs for a world where both comfort and security are abundant and no one need suffer a single pang of guilt. Every computer, every large dream house, and every new electronic gadget increases our power needs. Individually, each factor does not count for much. Taken together, the total produces a growing demand that is reflected in the power curve so tied to economic growth.

The dreamers would like to disconnect the two concepts— individual use and the overall power curve. They want their stuff, and they want it quite badly, but they do not want to feel any remorse. Thus, they conjure up ways to make it all possible. Needing only a fraction of a megawatt to power their own home, they envision a windmill that will provide all their electricity, and that for a few neighbors besides. They do not consider the cost of building hundreds of windmills to meet the power needs of their town. They do not consider what is necessary to generate electricity when the winds are calm. It is all very simple for the alarmists. Reality does not matter. They are convinced that they can have it all.

The electric companies have a different perspective. They have to provide the juice, regardless of the weather. Solar power is wonderful, but consumers will not pay a premium to the sun. Wind power is great, but much of the country cannot count on the wind nearly enough of the time. According to Department of Energy statistics, wind farms—on average—generate less than 20 percent of the power that they are capable of generating. Put another way, when one builds a windmill, one has to make sure that another form of reliable back-up power is available for at least 80 percent of the year.

What to do? Burning natural gas represents the most energy-efficient and environmentally friendly option available. Neither clouds nor winds will affect the ability of a utility to produce electrons at a reasonable price when they utilize gas technology. Inevitably, the power industry looked to natural gas as the solution to growing demand, but communities had been whipped into a frenzy by the environmental industry and a mainstream media sympathetic to their cause. People have grown ultrasensitive to any degree of risk and have been convinced that risk-free alternatives are readily available. Many continue to believe that alternate sources of power could fill all our energy needs, were it not for the evil oil companies conspiring with the government to suppress the technology that is supposedly so readily available. The truth, of course, is something else again.

The public at large does not realize how big the atmosphere is. Pollution from coal-fired power plants accounts for millions of tons a year of pollution. Those are frightening numbers, but they translate into only a fraction of a part per million once pollution is diluted by the sheer mass of the atmosphere. Natural gas burns far, far clearer than coal does. For an equivalent amount of power generated, the pollutants emitted when burning natural gas are a tiny fraction of those generated by coal. If we assume that increasing demand for power is not going to change—which it is not—the question becomes, How to generate that power most efficiently and cleanly? If we use gas instead of coal, the amount of pollution emitted goes down by a factor of more than 100 for the same amount of power produced.

So hooray for gas, right? Except that is not the way it has worked out. The climate of fear and environmental paranoia is such that even power plants burning natural gas face fierce opposition in many places. Communities see hundreds of tons of pollution attributed to natural-gas-fired power plants, and they react with horror. Few people seem to realize that a few hundred tons of air pollutants coming from burning natural gas often serve to replace tens of thousands of tons that coal stations would otherwise produce. Should an environmental crusader somehow happen to make the connection, it does not matter, for the environmental community is certain that the impossible alternatives will, somehow, fill the void instead.

The crusade against the power industry has been an ongoing battle, and the story of the peaker-plant boom that occurred a decade ago provides a good illustration of how that battle is fought. By the late 1990s, power demands had reached a critical stage throughout the nation. Increased demand led to waves of summer brownouts and, not unexpectedly, drove up the price of electricity. Entrepreneurs saw an opportunity to make money as the price of power soared. Thus, the so-called peaker-plant boom was born. Peaker plants were built to absorb electrical demand when it was at its highest, typically during hot summer workdays. Ideally, these plants would provide a quick burst of power, generating juice when it was needed and shutting down when night fell and demand decreased. They would also break the mold by providing smaller, regional sources of generation. Instead of building huge power plants generating thousands of megawatts, the new model provided for smaller plants, typically a few hundred megawatts in capacity, that would chiefly serve the immediate vicinity.

These two factors would make for a much more efficient power system. The big, utility-owned plants, mostly nuclear and coal-fired boilers, would provide a base load, the minimum amount of electricity needed all the time. Ready response by peakers would fill the gaps when more was needed. It was a system that made more sense, both economically and environmentally, than the previous setup. Before the peaker push, many utilities kept coal-burning plants on "hot-standby," with their boilers burning fuel but not actually generating power. Given the long start-up times for coal boilers, measured in hours, it was all they could do to ensure the reliability of the system.

Plants on hot-standby spent hundreds of hours polluting and wasting energy for no good purpose. Peaker plants allow utilities to end this practice and reap environmental benefit in two ways. Their quick response meant that marginal coal plants could shut down instead of waiting on standby. Furthermore, when the peakers did operate, they could use cleaner fuels to generate power.

This option brings us back to natural gas. Neither solar nor wind power is quick or reliable enough to respond to peak demand. Coal is too dirty and too slow. The only choice, all things considered, is turbines powered by natural gas. Natural-gas turbines are efficient, quick to respond, and about as clean burning as fossil fuel can get. Independent power producers flooded the turbine manufacturers with orders. General Electric and Westinghouse, later absorbed by Siemens, raked in the orders and the profits.

From a distance, the change in the market made perfect sense. Capitalism was working. Power demands rose, and the market responded by choosing the best option available to fill the need. However, that is the big picture. At the local level, the world often looked different. Communities did not see a massive, beneficial change in the way the nation's power was produced. All they saw was some damn profiteer rushing in to their community and trying to build a massive power plant that would emit hundreds of tons of pollution and kill their children. Community groups sprang up everywhere to oppose the new order. Local power generation was an invader in their eyes, and they fought back with every bit of panic and disinformation they could find.

Opponents pointed to the hundreds of tons of air pollution that peaker plants would emit and implied that the total amount would be deposited into the backyard of each and every local resident. It does not work that way, of course. Tailpipe emissions from a nearby road have much more effect on a given backyard than does a power plant sending gases far into the atmosphere. Nonetheless, in a climate of fear, the message of the panic-mongers struck a receptive chord.

Environmental groups were put in an awkward position. Some had actually issued position papers favoring gas-turbine technology prior to the peaker boom. Why would they not? In addition to being clean-burning, many turbines are much more efficient than any other fossil-burning technology. We will delve into physics and thermodynamics to explain why, which will undoubtedly cause many of you to flash back to the horrors of college science classes. Don't panic, dear readers. We will be gentle.

When one burns a fuel, it can generate power in one of two ways. One is by utilizing the heat produced, as in a boiler. One burns gas, oil, or coal to generate heat to make steam. Then the steam pressure spins an electric generator. The other way is to take advantage of the fact that fuel expands when it is burned. Car engines work this way. When gasoline explodes in a cylinder, it expands with enough power to move a piston, which ultimately turns the wheels of a Chevy. The unique thing about a particular class of gas turbines, called combined-cycle turbines, is that it takes advantage of both energy sources. Expanding gas makes the turbine spin, as in a jet engine. Then the hot gas exiting the back of the turbine is reused to make steam, which generates more power. It is a fantastically efficient arrangement. A typical coal boiler turns about 35 percent of the energy produced into power. For a combined-cycle gas turbine, that figure rises to over 50 percent efficiency.

If the nation really wants to achieve the dubious goal of reducing greenhouse-gas emissions, switching to combined-cycle gas turbines for electric production would more than do the trick. However, this goal is not realistic (albeit the folks at General Electric Power Systems would positively love to see it), but it serves to illustrate the point. Environmental groups should be thrilled with gas turbines. They are incredibly clean, and they reduce greenhouse gases. What's not to like?

The problem the explosion in turbine-powered plants put the environmental industry in a very awkward position. A particularly observant spectator might have noticed, for example, the amusing phenomena of Brian Urbaniczewski, of the American Lung Association (ALA), offering testimony both for and against the technology. When the State of Illinois considered new rules to restrict nitrogen oxide (NOx) emissions, Urbaniczewski argued that the regulations should favor gas-turbine technology over dirtier forms of energy production. However, when the same body considered a ban on turbines altogether, he was entirely in favor of eliminating the technology he had just supported. This author, present for both hearings, asked the ALA representative to explain his contradicting recommendations. The answer, Urbaniczewski explained, is that we all understand the science, but reality demands that ALA respond to its constituents. Such is the level of self-deception to which environmental groups have been reduced.

The theme would continue nationwide, where communities would respond to gas-turbine plants with the sort of fervor normally reserved for nuclear disposal facilities. Not surprisingly, the level of opposition was generally proportional to the prosperity of the community. When the town in question was relatively prosperous, the paranoia level was exceptionally high. Affluent towns were more aware of popular environmental myths and less likely to be swayed by the tax benefits that the plants would produce. Poorer communities, on the other hand, tended to welcome the facilities with open arms. They generated power, tax revenue, and a few jobs. Again, what's not to like?

In this case, to be sure, the system largely worked. Gas-turbine plants were built all over the country. Local opposition killed a few, in richer communities that needed the power worse than anyone, but that would be their problem in the years to come. Nationwide, the frequency of brownouts decreased. Yet that happy result occurred in spite of, not because of, the environmental industry and ignorant media coverage. The system worked—barely. Now, ten years after the peaker boom, placing and constructing new power plants is more difficult than ever. Indeed, as we shall see, the Obama administration is working to make it impossible to build any new fossil-fueled plant in America. We averted a power shortage in 2000, but should the economy recover and power demands rise again, it is difficult to believe that we can dodge the bullet again.

CHAPTER NINE

THERE'S NOTHING COOL ABOUT GLOBAL WARMING

THERE HAS BEEN MORE WRITTEN, BY MORE AUTHORS, about global warming than any other environmental issue in recent times. Despite Senator Harry Reid's 2009 declaration that a national cap-and-trade program is dead, climate change remains the current cause célèbre among environmentalists. The nation has responded to the supposed threat in ways that continue to reverberate throughout our economy. Individual states, working alone in some cases or as a part of regional partnerships in others, have made deep cuts in greenhouse-gas emissions and will continue to do so. Although more and more people believe that the global warming scare has been, at best, an embarrassing scientific blunder or, at worst, a deliberate hoax, the response of the states guarantees that America will continue to use less fossil fuel to generate power each year, no matter how abundant and cheap those fuels might be.

Can human activities actually alter the climate of the planet? Most scientists, on both sides of the debate, agree that they can. The difference is a matter of degree. So-called skeptical scientists maintain that our influence on the climate, compared to a myriad of other natural forces, is so small that it is really not worth worrying about. So-called alarmists, on the other hand, believe that the addition of a small amount of extra greenhouse gases to the atmosphere can upset a very delicately balanced system, and a series of cascading environmental effects will bring disaster. The question, as prominent global warming skeptic and climatologist Dr. Roy Spencer has said on many occasions, is, "How sensitive is [the] earth's climatic system?" Skeptics would answer that question "not very," while alarmists would say "extremely." In my opinion, having watched the debate unfold over the last twenty years, the "not very" answer is almost definitively the correct one. Work is still to be done, but a growing body of evidence says that the skeptics are right.

Until recently, the mainstream media almost never communicated that uncertainty. The popular press spent the better part of two decades trying to convince the public that mankind is causing irrevocable damage to the planet. Especially troubling is the fact that global warming proponents nearly shot down the debate. Officially, it was not supposed to be a debate at all. Favored scientists were given free reign by the press to voice their opinions, but those scientists who disagree with official dogma were dismissed out of hand by AP, Reuters, CNN, and their fellow news organizations. "Scientists agree," those organizations told us when global warming was the subject of a story. Actually, scientists were never in agreement.

The late Michael Crichton, in his novel *State of Fear*, tried to point out the analogies to the past. Historically, conventional wisdom has accepted "scientific truths" that were later proven to be nonsense. Hitler rose to power by riding the wave of the "science" of eugenics. At one time, a mysterious compound called "phlogiston" was commonly accepted as the source of fire, before oxygen was discovered. Doubt, Chrichton pointed out, is the surest guide toward truth. Yet, when it came to global warming, doubt was absolutely unacceptable to many people in the press and in politics. The tide has turned, but vast swathes of the populace still believe that challenging the theory of climate change is heresy. When he was running for president, Al Gore told voters they should ignore global warming dissenters. Rudy Baum, the editor of *CE News* ("CE" for chemical and engineering)—the magazine that represents the American Chemical Society—wrote that the issue was "too important" to allow for any debate among scientists. *CE News,* under Baum's leadership, has stubbornly refused to publish dissenting opinions for years, no matter how well-documented the research or how well-respected the researcher. The infamous "climategate" emails showed how leading global warming researchers knowingly tried to squelch the work of scientists who disagreed with them.

How can that be? How can scientists abandon the idea that dissent is healthy in this supposedly enlightened age? If we are supposed to care about the prospect of a melting planet, should we not also be concerned about the price to fix the supposed problem? If man were indeed killing the planet by generating energy, then the price of reducing energy consumption is, indeed, significant. Cutting greenhouse gas emissions means cutting power production, which makes power more expensive and affects the lives of poor people most of all. How can that not matter?

Above and beyond the economic and societal effects of the fix, there is something even more important at stake: the sanctity of the scientific method. The scientific method is the bedrock upon which all of mankind's technological progress is based. It is the framework for dispassionately establishing the truth among a host of theoretical constructs. Much like our legal system, reasonable doubt is at the heart of the scientific method. So long as there are good reasons to question a theory, the scientific community is supposed to welcome—even encourage—debate. Yet the mainstream media and political activists struggled mightily to quash debate about global warming, much in the manner that the Inquisition sought to silence Protestants; environmentalists have been about as successful in their quest. Even though climate-change advocates spent years claiming that there's nothing left to debate, and major media outlets parroted that position almost every day, dissenting, skeptical voices would not be silenced. Scientists and policymakers like Roy Spencer, Steve Milloy, Richard Lindzen, Joe Bast, and Lord Christopher Monckton are no longer voices in the wilderness; more and more people are beginning to understand that deeply flawed science that has led us down this road.

The theory of man-made global warming is usually presented in simplistic terms: man produces gases that retain the heat of the sun in the atmosphere, chiefly carbon dioxide and methane. Industrial activity—mostly power production and the combustion of gasoline in vehicles—is the source of these gases (although hardly the only sources since Mother Nature generates these gases as well). If we do not cut back on power production and build cars that sip (rather than guzzle) gas, the atmosphere will heat up, the ice caps will melt, and we are all doomed.

No responsible scientist disputes the fact that carbon dioxide, methane, and other gases can retain heat. The question is: How much does that effect matter? If the carbon dioxide in the atmosphere retained all of the heat it could, the temperature of the earth would be well over 200 degrees Fahrenheit. We are not frying eggs on our sidewalks, so we can safely assume that there are other factors at work. Cloud cover, ocean currents, and wind patterns have a big influence on temperatures, too. When considered in isolation, trace greenhouse gases, such as methane and carbon dioxide, have a marginal influence on climate. No scientist, whether skeptic or alarmist, would dispute that statement.

The true supposed power of carbon dioxide and methane does not arise from their ability to reflect heat themselves, but rather because—or so the theory goes—increased concentrations of these gases will lead to the evaporation of more water into the atmosphere. Because water vapor is a very powerful greenhouse gas, it is this effect—generically known as "feedback"—that supposedly leads to drastic climate change. In order to prove that greenhouse gases generated by human activity have substantial influence on temperatures, scientists use computer models. Even though the virtual world has increased by leaps and bounds over the past few decades, predicting the weather on a global basis is still an incredible challenge. A tweak here or a tweak there, and those incredibly complex models will yield vastly different results. Furthermore, these models do not account for everything that goes on in the atmosphere. Feedback can be positive (increasing temperatures), but it might also be negative (decreasing temperatures). For example, when we take into account that increased evaporation of water can also lead to increased cloud formation and that clouds tend to cool the surface of the earth, we are describing a negative feedback effect. Nonetheless, proponents of catastrophic climate change theory are certain—based solely on computer models—that feedback is strongly positive. The views of scientists on the other side of the argument range from saying that feedback is weakly positive to weakly negative.

Man-made greenhouse gases, in other words, do not act independently on the weather, and there are a wide variety of opinions about how significant a role they play at all. Man-made greenhouse gases are only a single factor, of relatively small effect, when compared with solar activity, ocean currents, cloud cover, wind patterns, and a number of other variables. Exactly what fractional influence greenhouse gases have on temperature in practice is the essence of the debate.

Proponents of global warming spend a lot of time selling the media "evidence" to prove their theory. Most all of it has been either disproven or can rationally be explained in other ways.

For example, the Holy Grail of global warming for many years was the so-called hockey stick graph. This chart purported to show an increase in the planet's temperature that neatly corresponded to an increase in atmospheric carbon dioxide concentrations in the industrial era. As independent researcher Steve McIntyre definitively proved, the hockey stick graph was a lie. The graph is a mathematical production, not a historical record. When McIntyre and other scientists delved into the formulas used to create the graph, they found that *any* set of base data would create the alarming chart. It was meaningless. Although the scientific community acknowledged the error, the mainstream media reported very little of the story until climategate happened.

Climate-change advocates also point to natural phenomena as proof that humans are destroying the planet. They claim that sea levels are rising as ice caps melt. They point to coastal erosion, melting glaciers, and catastrophic weather events as proof of the phenomena. There is little truth in any of these examples. At the most basic level, there is no good evidence to show that sea levels have changed appreciably over the last 100 years. Sea level is an enormously difficult phenomenon to measure in the first place, but the best of those studies indicates that sea levels have not changed much since the end of the last ice age, about 10,000 years ago. Coastal erosion? Sure, it is occurring. It always has and always will. It is part of the natural cycle, counterbalanced by that other vital piece of the puzzle: land creation. As the tides sweep away some coastal areas, the waves deposit silt to create new ones, and volcanoes belch lava to make even more land. Overall, the total land area on the globe is increasing, not decreasing, which is hardly consistent with the idea that the seas will flood us all.

The source of the purported global flood is, of course, what is described as the "ice caps." This is a misnomer. For all practical purposes, there is only a single ice cap: Antarctica. The South Pole holds about 95 percent of the planet's frozen water supply. Nonetheless, the amount of ice in Antarctica is increasing, not decreasing. It is true that the average amount of Arctic (North Pole) ice has decreased steadily, but—to the consternation of environmentalists—Arctic ice has been on the rebound since 2008. When Arctic ice cover was at a minimum, environmentalists bemoaned the fact that the famed Northwest Passage through northern Canadian waters was open for the first time in modern history. This, too, was a falsehood: there is ample documentation of ships traveling through the Northwest Passage in the 1930s, when Arctic ice was at a minimum yet again.

Interestingly, some national media outlets have acknowledged that the all-important Antarctic ice cap is growing. Yet, according to the environmentalists they interview, the increase in ice in the South Pole proves their theories correct once again. Why not? Everything else seems to. Environmentalists explain the growing Antarctic ice cap by saying that global warming is causing more precipitation, which results in more snowfall in Antarctica, leading to more ice. In sum, even though the planet is heating up, we still have more frozen water on its surface. It is a very odd world these people live in. They also point to every hurricane, cyclone, and tornado as proof of their theories. The response to this assertion is easy. According to historical records, the number and intensity of catastrophic weather events have not changed. Mother Nature is a violent old broad, but no more or less than ever.

Yet global warming remains a national issue. Because the economic and societal implications are so severe, it is one of the rare cases where Republicans have held their ground against hard-core environmentalists, which thoroughly annoys the latter. It is good that the GOP chose to make a stand on this issue, for even if one were to accept the theory that carbon dioxide emissions are a problem, the United States would not be the villain. A closer examination of the data shows that the United States is the target of a power play intended to wreck one of the most energy-efficient economies in the world.

Conventional wisdom says otherwise, of course. Conventional wisdom says that America is terribly wasteful, producing more carbon dioxide per person than any other nation on the planet, except China. Perhaps that is so, but is the amount of carbon dioxide emitted per person the true measure of waste? We produce stuff—food, products, medicines, and equipment—that is used across the planet. What if we were to measure our use of energy (and generation of carbon dioxide, which results from producing that energy) against our ability to produce the goods and services the world demands? The easiest way to do that is to compare carbon dioxide generation with economic activity, measured as Gross Domestic Product (GDP). By that standard, the United States is not wasteful and measures up very well, indeed. In terms of tons of carbon dioxide per dollar of GDP, the United States ranks among the most efficient nations on the planet, along with countries such as France and Japan, which use significantly more nuclear power than we do (and these emit zero carbon dioxide).

The least efficient nations? Not surprisingly, the Third World is terribly inefficient, with many of those nations generating two to three times more carbon dioxide per dollar of economic activity than the United States does. Among the most inefficient economies, three countries stand to gain more than any other should the Kyoto protocol, the Copenhagen accords, or other similar scheme be adopted in the United States: China, India, and Russia.

Under the terms of Kyoto, the Peoples Republic of China, India, and the Russian Federation would not have had to reduce a single ton of carbon dioxide emissions, despite the fact that the three are among the world's worst at making good use of power. When China and India were asked to join the United States in a commitment to make meaningful, verifiable greenhouse-gas reductions during the Copenhagen conference in 2010, both countries refused. With a huge advantage in the price of labor over the Western world, these nations would benefit enormously if the United States acted unilaterally. Their energy costs would remain stable, while the United States, forced to cut back on power, would see the price of production rise.

Reducing fossil fuel use in the United States, in short, would be the death knell of America's beleaguered manufacturing sector and a godsend for the trio of potential powerhouses. Russia, which has almost unlimited energy resources but a relatively small population, would become Asia's gas station to an even greater degree than it already is. With no restrictions on their production and competition from the West short-circuited by the effort to reduce greenhouse gas, the Russians would provide the power that China and India need. While American manufacturers bled themselves to a slow, painful death, industrial expansion in China and India would blossom.

With no artificial restrictions on productive capacity or transport options in these countries, their price of goods, relative to domestically manufactured items, would drop further.

Considered dispassionately, carbon-reduction schemes are a brilliant global power play. Through the clever use of one statistic, the framers of such proposals managed to create a mechanism that both (1) confirms what the rest of the world already *knows* (Americans are greedy, wasteful bastards who need to be stopped) and (2) hands American markets to Asia without having to wrestle with the inconvenience of capitalism and the free market. If a massive greenhouse-gas-reduction program is ever adopted by the United States and all that is predicted above comes to pass, the amount of carbon dioxide in the air will not go down one iota. In fact, it would rise. Look at the numbers:

SELECTED NATIONAL DATA (2007)		*SOURCE:* UN STATISTICAL DIVISION			
NATION	POPULATION (Thousands)	GDP (Millions U.S. Dollars)	CO_2 EMISSIONS (Thousands of Metric Tons)	CO_2 EMISSIONS PER PERSON (Tons/Person)	CO_2 EMISSIONS PER ECONOMIC OUTPUT (Tons/$1,000 GDP)
China	1,318,310	3,382,267	6,538,367	4.96	1,933.13
India	1,124,787	1,176,890	1,612,362	1.43	1,370.02
Russia	142,100	$1,290,082	1,537,357	10.82	1,191.67
Bolivia	9,518	13,120	13,190	1.39	1,005.34
Libya	6,156	58,333	57,334	9.31	982.87
Australia	21,015	820,974	374,045	17.80	455.61
US	301,920	13,751,395	5,838,381	19.34	424.57
Canada	32,976	1,329,883	557,340	16.90	419.09
Tanzania	41,276	16,825	6,043	0.15	359.17
Japan	127,771	4,384,252	1,254,543	9.82	286.15
Germany	82,268	3,317,366	787,936	9.58	237.52
France	61,707	2,589,841	371,757	6.02	143.54
World				4.2	

As economic activity moves east, the amount of carbon dioxide in the atmosphere would increase. The numbers tell us that every dollar that moves in that direction will generate from three to five times more carbon dioxide than the same economic activity in the United States. China's economic growth has been powered by a lot of coal, and that practice is not going to change anytime soon.

Should America ever implement a greenhouse-gas trading program on a national scale, the result would be a massive redistribution of wealth in this country. Trading programs are supposed to translate into free-market opportunities, which draw savvy capitalists to the market like shoppers to Walmart. We have got a bit of history with pollution-trading programs. Nationwide, power plants have been buying and selling sulfur dioxide emissions under the Acid Rain program for years. Regional trading schemes for other pollutants, such as Volatile Organic Compounds and nitrogen oxides, have also sprung up in recent times. These initiatives all provide object lessons in the economics of pollution. Although they are nominally called "free market" control of pollution, trading programs are ultimately controlled by the regulators. It takes a scholarly understanding of the subsystems of the system to know why.

Trading programs rely upon "emission allowances" to work. The regulatory authority will distribute these allowances (sometimes called "credits" in the vernacular) among industrial sources in what it perceives to be an equitable manner. The total distribution equals the targeted amount of emissions in the airshed as a whole. Thus, if the EPA wants to limit nitrogen oxide emissions in the Midwest to 1,000,000 tons per year, it will give 100,000 tons of credits to utility A, and 85,000 tons to utility B, and so on. The total amount of credits issued will not exceed 1,000,000 tons. The individual companies are then free to buy and sell their credits as needed. Theoretically, the free market will then determine which companies can control their emissions most economically. If the price of credits is high enough, utility A will find it profitable to put in more control than it needs and sell the excess to someone else.

It sounds fantastic in theory, but the initial allocation is the key to the program. Much like the Oklahoma land rush, how much one is able to claim at the outset makes all the difference in the long run. Consequently, the regulators come into the picture. In a trading program, the initial allocation of carbon dioxide credits has enormous economic import. The companies that understand how to play the game know to position themselves to grab as many credits as they possibly can. This initial distribution of pollution credits relies upon the regulations. The EPA looks at the rules and then allocates credits proportionally, based on the extent to which these companies comply with those rules. If company A is in full compliance, they get a full share of credits. Company B, in 80 percent compliance, gets an 80 percent allocation. Of course, the government gets its cut, too. The defunct Waxman-Markey bill, for example, would have made utilities pay for each credit, at a rate of 15 percent of the going market rate per credit allocated. That translates into big money for the U.S. government, which is why cap and trade is so often called cap and tax.

Given that the United States does not have any rules covering carbon dioxide emissions, the critical baseline distribution would essentially be up for grabs. At that point, the speculators come into the picture. They do their best to define what the baselines should be by looking for cases that should, in their view, equate to excess control, and then they buy up the credits they believe will amount to an excess in the future. Projects that involve wind power, biomass, and solar energy have thus become much more economically attractive, even without the government subsidies that drive so many of those projects. Speculators were betting on a cap-and-trade future, anticipating the profits to come at the expense of fossil-fueled power.

We can, and should, question the wisdom of entering into the biggest pollution-control program the world has ever seen, especially when it is based on questionable science and designed to reward inefficiency. Should this come to pass, no one should be deceived. Free markets are not really free in the environmental arena. The system will still depend on the regulators. They decide who has credits to trade and who will be forced to buy. Their rules determine how emissions are defined and verified. Trading programs may avoid hard limits on emissions, but they also require accountability, and the path to accountability runs directly through the bureaucrats.

Of course, trading programs are not a bad idea in every case. When they are used to reduce pollutants that are actually a legitimate concern (nitrogen oxides, for example), they provide manufacturers with more freedom. Ultimately, businessmen can choose between investing in more control technology or purchasing credits from other companies who already have done so. Thus we get the biggest bang for our environmental buck. However, we should not be fooled into thinking that trading programs take government out of the equation. Nothing could be further from the truth. The regulators may surrender the power to limit emissions at each plant, but they gain much more power by assuming the obligation to define those emissions and the amount of pollutants that are essentially *free* under the system.

Although it seems likely that environmentalists and their supporters in Congress will make another run at a national cap-and-trade scheme in the future, the irony is that the United States has already committed to making massive greenhouse-gas reductions. More than half of the states have adopted a Renewable Portfolio Standard (RPS). One regional cap-and-trade program is already in place, and two more are preparing to go on line. The net result of these programs will be a massive reduction in greenhouse-gas emissions nationwide, reductions that we have already begun to realize.

The RPS are programs enacted at the state level that direct utilities in the state to use less and less fossil fuel each year to generate power. New York's RPS, for example, mandates that no more than 71 percent of electricity used in the state can be generated using fossil fuels by the year 2015. In California, it is 67 percent by 2020; in New Jersey it is 77.5 percent by 2020. The list goes on, and other states are sure to establish their own RPS programs. These standards will go a long way to achieving what cap-and-trade was supposed to accomplish, as will regional cap-and-trade programs. A regional cap and trade program, the Regional Greenhouse Gas Initiative, is currently up and running on the east coast. Midwest and West Coast states will have their own programs operational soon, under the Midwest Greenhouse Gas Reduction Accord and the Western Climate Initiative, respectively.

The effect of such programs on the American economy has been and will continue to be damaging. The forms of renewable power that replace fossil fuels are more expensive, less reliable, and more difficult to maintain. We are paying a price to pursue a carbon-free nirvana.

Why do environmentalists not celebrate their triumph instead of continuing to paint America as the bad guy? America has done more to cut greenhouse-gas emissions than any other country. According to a study conducted by the Netherlands Environmental Assessment Agency, per capita emissions of greenhouse gases in the United States declined by 16 percent between 2000 and 2009. That reduction is almost 50 percent better than what the fifteen richest nations in Europe (the EU-15) could achieve in the same time frame, even though Europe has had a cap-and-trade program in place. Sadly, that particular statistic will not be cited on network news because it doesn't further the green agenda. Furthermore, when it comes to global warming, environmentalists and their supporters are committed to pushing an agenda, not publicizing facts.

CHAPTER TEN

MASS HYSTERIA: THE PRESS, POLLUTION, AND PARANOIA

UNDERESTIMATING THE ROLE THAT THE COMBInation of mainstream media and environmental groups plays in our overregulated society would be difficult. The two combine to create a climate of fear that often whips the public into a paranoid frenzy. Hyperbole often becomes the order of the day when environmental issues capture media attention. The slightest risks are blown out of all proportion, and hysterical parents are sure that their children will die unless the supposed "danger" is addressed. Politicians respond by granting regulators ever-increasing powers and loftier goals. Most of the environmental stories in the mainstream media—indeed, any stories that involve a combination of science and policy—are essentially indecipherable. The average reporter does not have the training to analyze technical issues independently, so reporters normally count on experts to explain the technicalities.

These experts, in turn, come in two types. There are environmental advocates who are, in the media's eyes, unbiased, selfless defenders of the public good. All opposing opinions and facts are supplied by people somehow connected to industry. This second group of experts, in the media's eyes, represents paid shills who are not to be trusted. In a typical mainstream media piece, environmental advocates "say" while industry representatives "claim." The difference is subtle but effective. The problem, of course is that the press is at least twenty years behind the times. Having been burned by the dark days of the Tobacco Institute and its clones, industry has grown careful. From a purely scientific point of view, their numbers hold up, in fact and in intent, much more often than not.

The mainstream media is blissfully unaware that environmental groups represent an industry, too, a multibillion-dollar industry, in fact. Worse, the environmental industry depends on fear to sell its product. No matter how much environmental progress we've made, the industry cannot afford to admit it, especially when Republicans are in power. Should environmentalists ever do so, they know that all the suburban housewives and Hollywood do-gooders would close their checkbooks. The environmental industry was born of crisis, and it depends on crisis to sustain it. The press does its worst damage when covering the sidestream issues. The big debates, global warming and new air-quality standards, at least attract some semblance of openness. The stories may be slanted, and they are, but at least opposing opinions are part of the debate.

Other stories fly below the radar and, consequently, are accepted with much less debate, if any. Consider the continuing argument over the use of bisphenol A (BPA), an ingredient found in a variety of plastics. Increasingly, environmental groups are calling for a ban on the use of BPA, and the Obama administration seems ready to oblige. Yet, the debate about the supposed toxic risk associated with BPA stretches back over the course of years, as environmental groups have slowly but surely been driving home the "truth" that BPA is dangerous, to the point that many Americans accept that point of view as a given. What follows are some excerpts from a story penned by Maggie Fox, a health and science correspondent for Reuters, on March 31, 2003:

WASHINGTON (Reuters). A common ingredient used to make plastics such as baby bottles causes birth defects in mice—defects that could also occur in people, U.S. researchers said on Monday.

They urged more research into the potential effects of bisphenol A, a chemical long criticized by environmentalists as being a hormone disruptor that could cause defects in embryos.

The defects they found, when they occur in humans, can cause miscarriages or mental retardation such as Down Syndrome—and they seem to be caused at what were considered to be low levels of exposure, the researchers report in the journal *Current Biology*.

After more of the same sort of alarmism, Fox adds:

While the study says nothing about the effects of bisphenol A in humans, Hunt said there is reason to believe they would be similar. The changes in the mice cause aneuploidy—a misalignment of the chromosomes that is seen in human birth defects and miscarriages.

"You don't wait to prove that it does that in people before you take some regulatory action," Vom Saal said, adding that he hopes Congress may now agree to fund more studies on the effects of bisphenol A.

"We are talking about these mice essentially drinking out of old baby bottles," Vom Saal said—noting that hard plastic containers like bottles start leaching bisphenol A when they begin to look cracked or etched.

He urged the chemical industry to make more plastic products that do not contain bisphenol A.

Some of the funding for the study came from the industry-supported American Chemistry Council via the National Institute for Environmental Health Sciences.

Nowhere in Fox's report, which was supposed to be a straight news story, did she present opposing data or opinions. Discussion of risk, or indeed proof of actual harm, is not offered. The reader can only conclude that bisphenol A is a deadly hazard, poised to kill our children. The actual science tells us something else again. Let us start with the big picture. Infant mortality rates in the United States are among the lowest in the world. Life spans are among the longest. If biophenol A is such a dire public-health threat, where are the bodies? Ms. Fox's story does not hold up on the microscopic level, either. The data tying bisphenol A to cancer is tenuous at best. It is another one of those cases, like Alar, in which one has to completely ignore the dose to prove any semblance of risk. Yes, if one consumes massive amounts of the chemical, thousands of times greater than one would ever be exposed to in real life (and if one is a rat), one might be in danger. Maybe.

Another common theme of mainstream media stories about the environment is the idea that America is so polluted—especially in the wake of the environmentally disastrous Bush administration—that merely drinking tap water or breathing the air is dangerous. The theme has not changed for years, despite the fact that the amount of pollutants of all kinds in the environment in the United States, including toxic pollutants, has steadily dropped over the course of the last forty years. Let us go back to Maggie Fox again, as she offers her sledgehammer touch to another story, once again involving that classic combination: infants and chemistry. Babies, she tells us in this July 14, 2005, story, are born awash in toxic chemicals:

WASHINGTON (Reuters). Unborn U.S. babies are soaking in a stew of chemicals, including mercury, gasoline byproducts and pesticides, according to a report to be released

Thursday. Although the effects on the babies are not clear, the survey prompted several members of Congress to press for legislation that would strengthen controls on chemicals in the environment.

The report by the Environmental Working Group is based on tests of 10 samples of umbilical cord blood taken by the American Red Cross. They found an average of 287 contaminants in the blood, including mercury, fire retardants, pesticides, and the Teflon chemical PFOA.

"These 10 newborn babies . . . were born polluted," said New York Rep. Louise Slaughter, who planned to publicize the findings at a news conference Thursday.

"If ever we had proof that our nation's pollution laws aren't working, it's reading the list of industrial chemicals in the bodies of babies who have not yet lived outside the womb," Slaughter, a Democrat, said.

Cord blood reflects what the mother passes to the baby through the placenta.

"Of the 287 chemicals we detected in umbilical cord blood, we know that 180 cause cancer in humans or animals, 217 are toxic to the brain and nervous system, and 208 cause birth defects or abnormal development in animal tests," the report said.

Blood tests did not show how the chemicals got into the mothers' bodies.

MERCURY AND PESTICIDES

Among the chemicals found in the cord blood were methyl mercury, produced by coal-fired power plants and certain industrial processes. People can breathe it in or eat it in seafood, and it causes brain and nerve damage.

Also found were polyaromatic hydrocarbons, or PAHs, which are produced by burning gasoline and garbage and which may cause cancer; flame-retardant chemicals called polybrominated dibenzodioxins and furans; and pesticides including DDT and chlordane.

The same group analyzed the breast milk of mothers across the United States in 2003 and found varying levels of chemicals, including flame retardants known as PBDEs. This latest analysis also found PBDEs in cord blood.

The Environmental Working Group report coincided with a Government Accountability Office report issued Wednesday that said the Environmental Protection Agency does not have the powers it needs to fully regulate toxic chemicals.

The GAO, the investigative arm of Congress, found that the EPA's Toxic Substances Control Act gives only "limited assurance" that new chemicals entering the market are safe and that the EPA only rarely assesses chemicals already on the market.

"Today, chemicals are being used to make baby bottles, food packaging, and other products that have never been fully evaluated for their health effects on children—and some of these chemicals are turning up in our blood," said New Jersey Democrat Sen. Frank Lautenberg, who plans to co-sponsor a bill to require more testing of toxic chemicals.

Pollutants and other chemicals are believed to cause a range of illnesses. But scientists agree the only way to really sort out the effects is to measure how much gets into people and then see what happens to their health.

Once again, Fox is fascinating for what she did not tell us. She offers no proof that would link the supposed toxic soup to actual harm. For good reason: there is none. She did not compare the levels of those elements that occur naturally in the body, such as lead and mercury, to current levels. She did not bother to consider concentrations at all. There are no numbers in the Fox story. To her, a toxin is clearly a toxin, no matter what the dose. But that is not the way it actually works. Toxins are defined by dose. Minute concentrations of "toxins" occur, and have always occurred, in the body. Their occurrence is natural. We have always carried elements such as mercury, lead, and arsenic around with us. Finding them is no big deal. The issue is how much is present, and that question is something Maggie Fox and so many similar journalists are just not going to answer.

On September 23, 2008, the *Chicago Tribune*'s Michael Hawthorne and Darnell Little authored a "Tribune Watchdog Report" under the bold headline "Chicago's Toxic Air." According to the authors, "People living in Chicago and nearby suburbs face some of the highest risks in the nation for cancer, lung disease, and other health problems linked to toxic chemicals pouring from industry smokestacks, according to a Tribune analysis of federal data."

A *Tribune* analysis of any sort these days is about as worthwhile as a Hugo Chavez probe into Venezuelan voting irregularities, but Hawthorne and Little were sure they were right. They discovered a USEPA database, the Risk-Screening Environmental Indicators (RSEI) model, to be exact (you can almost hear them yelling "gotcha!"), and they came to an alarming conclusion after poking around a bit. "Those who look up Cook County will see it ranked worst in the nation for dangerous air pollution, based on 2005 data." The *Tribune* also found Chicago was among the ten worst cities in the United States.

There is so much that is overstated and just plain wrong about those conclusions, and about the article in general, that it is impossible to point it all out. Let us consider a couple of points. Hawthorne and Little clearly did not understand what they were looking at, as they pored, wide-eyed, through the data. At the most basic level, the RSEI model only accounts for industrial sources of pollution, yet industry contributes only about one-fourth of the air pollution in an urban area such as Chicago. Therefore, one cannot conclude that Chicago's air is "among the worst" using RSEI data, because one would not be looking at anything close to the entire picture. As a matter of fact, big industrial sources (the plants with tall smokestacks) have relatively little effect locally, because their emissions disperse far and wide.

The reporters also did not notice that the RSEI data is based on another data set, the Toxics Release Inventory, which does not account for all polluters, but only a select group, further limiting this

already limited universe. Such information about the origin and limi-
tation of the data is published at the RSEI website, but few reporters
are going to take the time to understand the nuances of such a data
set. Rather than relying on a screening tool, the more accurate way
to assess risk in a case like this is to see what is actually in the air we
breathe, rather than considering the emissions from one particular
subset of sources that contribute to air quality. USEPA operates a
network of more than 5,000 ambient air monitors across the nation
in order to do exactly that, to let people know how clean the air is in
their community. Many of these monitors are dedicated to measuring
air toxins in the air we breathe. There are more than 180 toxic air pollutants indentified by USEPA. Of these, some of the most significant
in an urban setting are formaldehyde and benzene (emitted by cars
and trucks for the most part) and lead. "Fine" particulate, although
not classified as a toxin, is also a health concern in most big cities.

According to USEPA's actual monitors (not models), Cook
County ranked 116th (out of 198 sites) for formaldehyde, 60th (out
of 195) for lead, 128th (out of 366) for benzene, and 80th (out of
1,135) for fine particulate, in a nationwide comparison of monitoring
site. Far from being the toxic wasteland that the *Chicago Tribune*
depicted, Chicago is a very average city in terms of air pollution,
better than some and worse than others. Moreover, as is the case
across the country, the amount of toxins in Chicago's air has dropped
and will probably continue to do so.

When the mainstream media covers environmental issues, they
take their cue from environmental groups. As alternative media outlets have grown in number and importance, environmental groups
themselves have stepped out from behind the curtain in increasing
numbers to push their agenda in a variety of blogs and news sites.
A piece that appeared on August 20, 2010, at the *Huffington Post*,
authored by Trip Van Noppen, president of Earth Justice, offers a
typical example. Commenting on proposed new rules that will affect
boilers burning fossil fuels (coal, oil, and natural gas), Van Noppen
wrote:

Coal-fired power plants are the largest industrial source of mercury and global warming pollution in the nation. They also are major sources of pollution that leads to smog and the contamination of water by heavy metals. Getting these facilities to follow the law and clean up will require an engaged public, so we'll be calling on you—our supporters—many times between now and the end of 2012 to join us in advocating for strong rules.

When Van Noppen urges readers to get coal-fired power plants "to follow the law," the clear implication is that coal-fired power plants are not currently following the law. This is false. The issue he is raising is the push to change regulations to make emissions limits more stringent. When and if such new limits are promulgated by the EPA, operators of coal-fired power plants will have a period to comply with the new rules. If, at the end of that time, they cannot meet the limits, the operators would not be following the law. As the law currently stands, however, the vast majority of power plants are following it.

Van Noppen also says that these plants are "major sources of pollution" and the the largest industrial source of mercury and global warming pollution." Again, the Earth Justice president is being disingenuous, at best. These plants are indeed "major sources" of pollution, in that most of the plants affected by the proposed rule emit more than 100 tons per year of one or more pollutants, thus meeting the USEPA's definition of a "major source." However, this particular rule covers industrial, as opposed to utility, boilers. Industrial boilers are used at manufacturing facilities, such as oil refineries, ethanol plants, and food-production facilities. They are, as rule, far smaller than the big utility boilers that generate electricity; therefore, they emit far less pollution. Compared to utility boilers and to cars and trucks, industrial boilers are not a "significant" source of air pollution; they are a relatively minor player. When Van Noppen tries to imply that this rule is vital to cleaning up the air further, he is simply wrong. Like so many within the environmental community, either he does not understand the issue or he chooses to misrepresent it for his own purposes.

The rule in question would, if promulgated, create draconian limitations, and many in industry believe compliance would be impossible and would offer very little environmental return. At a time when we can least afford it, at a time when America's industrial sector is struggling to survive a recession and increased competition from China and India, the EPA would impose limits that would force a Hobsonian choice on many plants: operate legally in another country that does not have such ludicrous limits, or operate in the United States and pay penalties for being out of compliance with a rule they cannot follow.

As bad as national media sources and environmental groups can be, local news sources and environmental groups can be even worse. The peaker-plant boom attracted some of the most inflammatory rhetoric of the new century. At that time, for example, a California environmental-group publication called "Terrain" said that building clean-burning, natural-gas-fired peaker plants in response to California's energy crisis amounted to "environmental apartheid." The group shrieked that peaker plants would emit "two to twelve times more nitrogen oxides" per megawatt than conventional plants would, and plants would be built in minority neighborhoods in disproportionate numbers, exposing those populations to undue environmental risks. None of it was true. Gas-fired turbines, as we have seen, are the cleanest form of fossil-burning energy available. The emissions that are generated by these units disperse far from the host neighborhood.

In Illinois, the Sierra Club at least admitted that peaker plants are "much less polluting than coal." Still, the Club needed something to create panic, so it turned from the air to the water. The group urged their constituents to tell the governor to "stop granting permits for new peaker plants until new air and water protections are in place." The fact that the peaker plants would improve air quality and few would even use much water did nothing to allay the group's panic.

A local environmental group in the Milwaukee area seized upon the fear to raise an even more frightening spector, death by fireball. Even though propane is stored in quantity throughout the United States as a back-up fuel, a Wisconsin group called Citizen Power, Incorporated, found it especially troubling that a peaker plant would store propane to use in the event of a natural-gas shortage. "How much of New Berlin [Wisconsin] and surrounding communities would be destroyed by an accidental explosion of the 210,000 pounds of liquid propane that will be stored on site as a back-up fuel is anyone's guess," the group cried.

Actually, the answer is not a guess. Liquid propane does not explode, it burns. For 210,000 pounds of liquid propane to explode, it first has to vaporize into a gas, and then someone has to provide a spark for the cloud. The chances of the two events happening—which would require someone to provide a heat source to evaporate the propane—are infinitesimally small. However, most citizens would never know this if they read Citizen Power's propaganda.

Cell towers scare some people, for reasons that make no sense. The amount of radiation that one is exposed to from a cell-phone tower is far less than what one is exposed to in the course of an ordinary airplane flight or even sitting out in the sun and working on a tan. Nonetheless, the myth persists: cell towers are dangerous. "There is a growing body of scientific evidence that the electromagnetic radiation they emit, even at low levels, is dangerous to human health," the Mount Shasta Bioregional Ecology center warned its patrons. Not really. The body of scientific evidence says that cell towers are no more dangerous than sitting close to a TV. However, they are big, they are scary, and they are new..They represent progress, and, from an environmental group's point of view, they must be opposed.

The above is but a few—a very few—examples of how badly the press and environmental groups play fast and loose with the truth. A public that is largely scientifically uneducated counts on the media and environmental groups to explain the science to them. Sadly, both the media and environmental organizations have betrayed that trust again and again, creating an atmosphere where regulators are free to run wild.

CHAPTER ELEVEN

THE HOME FRONT

THE NATION'S MASSIVE PILE OF ENVIRONMENTAL regulations is a gold mine for the individuals and groups who do not want anything to ever change. Call them NIMBYs (Not in My Back Yard), BANANAs (Build Absolutely Nothing, Anywhere, Near Anyone), or NOPEs (Not on Planet Earth). They all want the same thing: the status quo, now and forever. Environmental rules are a convenient and effective tool they can use to accomplish that end. Someone wants to build a factory near your house? It will destroy the community's groundwater table. A new gas station is planned for a commercial strip down the street? Gas fumes and automobile exhausts will poison the air. A farmer wants to sell to a residential developer? Precious wetlands will be destroyed. With all of the checks, balances, and detailed analyses in place these days, finding any truth in any of the complaints is exceedingly rare. No matter. In the politics of opposition, quantity counts far more than quality. Every page in the federal register and in state regulations represents the opportunity for alarmists to generate another piece of waste material that might conceivably stick to the wall and raise a stink.

About this agenda, nothing is new. When the Romans built their first aqueduct, no doubt there was somebody with a villa in the hills who bitched to the Roman senate about the destruction of their view. The objective has never changed; we have simply given people more tools to achieve their goal. The effect of the environmental weapon at the local level can be profound, depending on the community. To understand why, let us consider a tale of two Illinois cities: Bartlett and Robbins.

Bartlett is a suburb on the far west side of Chicago. For most of its history, it has been an isolated, pastoral community. With a population that did not exceed the 20,000 mark until the 1990s and plenty of farmland and forest preserves between it and urban streetscapes, Bartlett long considered itself a hidden gem, and rightfully so. The 1990s brought economic and demographic expansion to Chicago, as it did for most urban areas. The suburban checkerboard extended, until developers noticed the village with good rail access and a quaint hometown feel. Homebuyers did, too. Bartlett's population doubled, and kept growing. The vast majority of new homebuyers were young, upwardly mobile, and looking for a quiet, good-quality home at a nice price possibly close to the center of metropolitan Chicago.

Some of those new residents defined the old joke: "Question: How much development is too much? Answer: Anything that's built after my house is finished." When a couple purchased a 3,000-square-foot home that overlooked a farmer's quiet corn field, they figured the corn would be there forever. "They wanted people to continue to own that land, and to keep it as open space for them," one Bartlett resident said about the NIMBYs in his town. "I'd like to have a 140-acre backyard that somebody else would pay to maintain for me, too, but that's not the way it works."

Most communities employ planners, either in-house if the community is big enough, or on a consulting basis if it is not. Today, eventual land use is charted out well before bulldozers and the carpenters turn a farm into a subdivision. It does not seem to make much difference whether the community proactively tries to let residents in on the plan or keeps relatively quiet. Families move in and out so quickly that few seem to catch on. "Planning is very much putting together a puzzle," veteran Streamwood, Illinois, planner Sharon Caddigan said. "Government is slow in the first place, and public planning is very, very slow. That hasn't changed, and it will never change."

Among the planning community, people expect opposition from neighbors. New developments inevitably go through a local public process in which residents have a chance to air their concerns and objections. That process can be painful, which leads to an inside joke among community planners. They know that hearings are over when the "five objectives" have been heard:

1. This project will kill my children.
2. This project will generate too much traffic (which will kill my children).
3. This project will flood my home.
4. This project will devalue my property.
5. This project will bring an end to human existence and all that is good—especially my children.

These are just excuses, of course. How much the alarmists actually believe their own propaganda is a matter of conjecture. Whatever the answer, environmental issues have now become an important component of the five objectives.

Consider a new gas station that was proposed in Bartlett in late 1990s. A town growing as fast as Bartlett would naturally be attractive to oil companies. All these people needed gas for all their SUVs. An entrepreneur found an attractive spot on a main road that was zoned commercial, agreed to a price with the landowner, and filed his plans with the village. The station's prospective neighbors hated it. The station would destroy their homes, they said. They cited the big five objectives, enhancing their position with claims that the gasoline tanks would leak and destroy their drinking water, fumes from cars would poison their kids, and the whole place would probably explode anyway. In fact, with modern underground storage-tank standards (double walls, with extensive leak detection), risk of groundwater contamination was slight, and the wells were far away in any case. Fumes from cars at the station would have almost zero effect on local air quality (which was good, as compared to the nearby main thoroughfare and background pollutants in the airshed). Furthermore, gasoline stations blow up much less often than homes do from—very rare—natural-gas leaks. But no matter how silly the arguments, the village felt an obligation to this noisy minority of residents. They said no to the entrepreneur. This would lead to significant problems for the village of Bartlett.

Property owners still have rights. Granted, those rights are decreasing, but they still exist in some form. When people invest in land that the municipality has designated for commercial development in the town's plan, the village cannot suddenly pull the rug out from under them. Thus, the village was sued. The property owner figured he was being denied the profit to which he was entitled. The village plan said that the location was supposed to be commercial. This was an approved, low-impact commercial use. How could the village block the sale? The developer felt that Bartlett had changed the rules in the middle of the game. The town spent more than six figures in legal fees and untold amounts of soft dollars in time the village staff took to respond to the suit. In the end, the village lost, as it should have.

In 2000, another development hit Bartlett that would, in some residents' minds, lead to the sort of Armageddon that a mere gas station could not create. A company wanted to build a power plant in town. Electric power lines crossed a natural-gas supply line on the western edge of the village. In the brave new world of environmentally responsible energy production, it was an ideal spot for a power plant. Gas turbines located at the spot could produce electricity with a minimum of infrastructure costs and maximum efficiency. European power giant ABB Raymond jumped at the opportunity. They bought land in Bartlett's westside industrial park and developed plans for a 1,500-megawatt power plant. At first, nobody noticed.

"It started out very quietly, though I didn't think the village would admit that," said Cindy Lenart, who covered the proceedings for the local newspaper, the *Bartlett Examiner*. "Once people figured out what was going on, they came out. The village moved their meetings to the high school, and probably 150 people came out to each meeting." Some of those people were calm and reasonable, but many of them were simply furious and refused to be placated. The power plant represented the end of the world. No stone would be left unturned when it came to arguing their case. One resident screamed that the proposed power plant would be another Chernobyl, though he failed to point out exactly where the plant would utilize nuclear material. A Bartlett mother choked back her tears as she predicted that the plant would kill all her children. In reality, burning natural gas and sending the byproducts of that combustion high into the atmosphere would have little effect on the town. From a local perspective, the plant would have far less of an effect on air quality than traffic would. From a regional and national perspective, it would only improve things—not that such mundane facts mattered. Paranoia usually conquers all.

After extensive hearings at the local level and an unprecedented number of reviews by the Illinois Environmental Protection Agency, the project was ultimately approved. Given their unpleasant experience with Citgo and the $400,000 per year in revenue that the power plant would bring in, town fathers and mothers had little reasonable choice. Contrast Bartlett's experience to that of Robbins, Illinois, a suburb to the south of Chicago.

Robbins is a small, impoverished and largely African-American suburb. Without much of a tax base, the village struggled to improve its services and infrastructure in order to attract more business and industry and, by extension, more revenue. However, they faced a catch-22: without better services and infrastructure, the town could not get the businesses that would generate these tax dollars. In the late 1990s, the town hit upon a unique solution: they would build a municipal waste incinerator.

Municipal waste incinerators are an especially efficient way of disposing of refuse. They reduce the volume of refuse by a factor of ten or more, leaving inert ash that is sent to landfills. They can generate a bit of energy, too. The environmental effects? A modern, properly engineered waste incinerator has much less effect on the populace and environment than an average expressway does. Nonetheless, municipal waste incinerators have become a cause célèbre among environmental groups. Organizations like the Sierra Club, the Environmental Defense Fund, and National Resources Defense Council use scare tactics to convince residents that locating a municipal waste incinerator in their community is a death sentence.

They focus on the toxic byproducts that may be produced—by anyone burning anything—and never, ever talk about how the concentrations of those pollutants compare to actual risk levels. In fact, the biggest risk of inhaling airborne toxins the average person faces is when they light up their backyard barbecue, which is to say that there is not much risk at all. People in Robbins examined the science, took a look at their needs, and reached an entirely reasonable conclusion: let us build a municipal waste incinerator in our town. Such a facility could serve as a regional center for waste disposal, generating large amounts of much-needed tax revenue. Robbins invited—emphasis on "invited"—a trash-to-cash plant into town.

The environmentalists were furious. A municipal waste incinerator? In a poor community? They were appalled. "Environmental injustice!" they cried, conveniently forgetting that Robbins had asked for the plant, not had it forced upon them. Through years of hearings at the local and state levels, the two sides debated the issue. Eventually, the plant was approved and built and began operation in 1997 as Robbins Resource Recovery. Yet the environmental groups' opposition to the project did not cease. They continued to lobby legislators, hoping to have the plant closed. They cited permit violations, painting the facility as an environmental disaster.

In fact, the facility was indeed cited by the Illinois EPA for permit violations, but those exceedences were very technical in nature and did not endanger human health or the environment. Robbins Resource Recovery made the mistake of accepting permit limits that were far more stringent than the law required. Thus, every time it exceeded these limits—even for a second—it was a "violation" even though the facility was emitting no more air pollution than others that had permits that conformed with applicable regulations, rather than going far beyond them. No matter. Environmental groups eventually convinced enough legislators in Illinois that Robbins Resource Recovery represented a clear and imminent danger. The Illinois General Assembly took action that did not directly shut down the plant but made it impossible for the facility to make money. In 2000, the plant was shut down, a move that nearly bankrupted its owner, Foster Wheeler Corporation, and—more important—decimated the village of Robbins that badly needed the revenue the plant had been providing. In the years to come, Robbins could not afford to fix water mains, pay police officers, or perform a host of other basic functions of local government. Environmental groups failed to notice as they moved on to richer pastures.

Advocacy groups often play the environmental-justice card, claiming that low-income, minority neighborhoods are subject to more pollution than more affluent areas. How true, or how significant that claim is, should be a matter of debate. In these examples at least, it is difficult to see how justice was done. Bartlett, an upscale community with a history of open debates, approved the idea of a 1,500-megawatt power plant with sparse opposition from environmental groups. Robbins, a struggling town that asked to build a lower-impact project was denied the chance to improve itself, largely because environmental groups made the project the object of a propaganda war. Where exactly is the justice in that?

The most significant way in which environmental rules can affect communities may be one of the most hidden. Environmental excuses can occlude the big picture. Communities and industry pay the price, and nobody in government seems to notice. Democrats side with the extremists because they are a natural part of the Democratic constituency. For Republicans, the issue is a bit more complex, even if the result is usually the same. The GOP generally knows that environmental regulations are excessive, but little is to be gained politically from fighting the trend. The number of voters who understand the situation, much less care about it, is depressingly low.

Accordingly, environmental regulation ranks very low on the list of Republican priorities. Republicans generally treat environmental policy as a throwaway, often passing massive regulatory programs into law as a means of showing that they can be progressive, too. Not that such acquiescence does them any good. The GOP could ban the internal combustion engine, and Sierra Club would still chastise them for not regulating emissions from the horse-drawn carriages that remain.

CHAPTER TWELVE

WILDER THAN EVER BEFORE

O F THE MANY REASONS THAT BARACK OBAMA WAS elected president in 2008, arguably the biggest factor was that he was not George W. Bush. Right or wrong, the backlash against Bush and his administration's policies reached a fever pitch by the end of the president's second term. The race between John McCain and Barack Obama became a contest to show which candidate could be the least like Bush and, as expected, the senator from Illinois won. The environmental arena is one of the many policy areas in which President Obama is trying to show his supporters that he is not George W. Bush. As we have seen, George W. Bush actually did what every president since Nixon has done: he continued to reduce pollution in the United States and advanced environmental policies. Because environmental groups refuse to acknowledge this and because the green movement is a part of the Obama coalition, the new president has naturally pursued more aggressive environmental policies than his predecessor did.

Every administration does it, but the policies that President Obama, his EPA administrator Lisa Jackson, and energy czar Carol Browner have pursued go far beyond anything that we have ever seen in America. For the first time in history, designing environmental policy has become virtually the sole purview of academics and environmentalists. In the past, new regulations and policies were almost always the result of compromise. The USEPA duly considered input from everyone—including industry—before promoting new rules. Inevitably, the rules did not fully satisfy everyone, but they managed to keep the ball of environmental progress rolling. Now, under the new regime, industry is a stakeholder in the process in name only. For all practical purposes, the Obama administration has committed itself to following the most radical courses available, the policies that extremists in academia and environmental groups advocate. The economic impact of these policies is going to be more damaging than anyone can imagine. While the USEPA blithely assures us that these policies will, in fact, save money—chiefly because people will supposedly get sick far less often if they are adopted—the agency is whistling in the dark as it pushes the nation to an abyss that will consume our already beleaguered industrial sector. Some old-timers within the EPA will admit as much privately, although never publicly; they need their jobs and their pensions too much to speak out.

There are numerous examples of the recent regulatory piling on. The situation has gotten so bad that one state regulator solemnly declared, "You can build any kind of a plant you want these days—so long as it emits nothing." That keen-witted remark is only slightly removed from the truth. The Obama administration is not only pushing unachievable, costly environmental rules; it is also creating many new rules. If industry had a hard time keeping up with the flood of regulations previously, they cannot possibly weather the tsunami of regulation this administration has created. Let us consider a few examples.

NEW CLEAN-AIR STANDARDS

In 2010, the United States Environmental Protection Agency announced plans to lower its standard for urban ozone, popularly known as smog, to a level between 60 and 70 parts per billion. This move would be the fourth such reduction since the implementation of the Clean Air Act in the 1970s. The original standard was 120 parts per billion, a goal that was reduced under the Clinton administration to 80 parts per billion in 1997. It was then further reduced under the Bush administration to 75 parts per billion in 2008. The Clinton-era reduction in the smog standard was widely hailed among environmental groups, although the further reduction during the Bush administration was roundly criticized by those same groups.

"Using the best science to strengthen these standards is a long overdue action that will help millions of Americans breathe easier and live healthier," USEPA administrator Lisa Jackson said in a press release. The "best science" refers to the advice of the EPA's Clean Air Scientific Advisory Committee (CASAC), a purportedly independent board of scientists who participate in the process of setting increasingly stringent definitions of clean air. However, USEPA is not supposed to base its decisions solely on CASAC's recommendations. According to the EPA, the "scientific community, industry, public interest groups, the general public, and the Clean Air Scientific Advisory Committee (CASAC)" all get to play a role whenever the agency sets new standards. That formula, which every president from Nixon through Bush has employed, has been effectively discarded by the Obama administration, which has chosen to defer to CASAC alone.

The fact that CASAC picked the lowest proposed standard as the best proposed standard should come as no surprise. Of the seven CASAC members, four are engineers, modelers, and one ecosystems analyst—and all four are wholly unqualified to opine on issues regarding public health. The remaining three have a vested interest in seeing lower smog standards: all are academics whose research funding depends on air-pollution alarmism. CASAC chair Dr. Jonathan Samet, for example, has spent a great deal of his professional career decrying secondhand smoke, and he is also an advisor to the American Lung Association (ALA), an organization that spends a great deal of time and money lobbying for increasingly restrictive smog standards. Another CASAC member, Dr. Helen Suh MacIntosh, was once a Q&A columnist for treehugger.com.

The EPA estimated the cost of implementing new smog standards at $19 to $90 billion, but the agency hastens to add that the benefits will total $13 to $100 billion. The benefits consider only avoided costs, in terms of reduced medical care, worker productivity (due to a reduction in sick days), and the like. Factors such as increased unemployment—the result of reduced profit margins in the manufacturing sector—and the increased cost of goods and services associated with a tighter standard were not part of the analysis. Further, when estimating the cost of compliance, the EPA acknowledged that it factors in the unknown cost of installing controls that have not yet been invented.

One of the main reasons that the EPA and organizations like ALA advocate this new, drastically more stringent standard is that it will, they say, prevent childhood astuma and other forms of asthma. In the last thirty years, data compiled by the National Center for Health Statistics indicates that childhood asthma has increased by more than 150 percent. However, in that same period, according to USEPA monitoring data, smog concentrations have decreased by 25 percent nationwide.

If adopted, the new smog standards will significantly increase the cost of living for millions of Americans. They will be forced to purchase special (and therefore more expensive) low-vapor-pressure formulations of gasoline. Vehicle-inspection programs, ubiquitous in large metropolitan areas, will spread to midsize cities. Remotely located power-generation facilities, heretofore untouched by smog rules, will have to install and maintain expensive, new control systems and will pass that cost along to consumers. Perhaps most distressing of all, the beleaguered American manufacturing sector, which has so far managed to escape the most painfully expensive requirements of clean-air regulation, will face new mandates that will make it even more difficult to compete against plants overseas that are not similarly constrained.

However, for the Obama administration, there is nothing to lose. At the absolute earliest, the new smog standard will require industry compliance in 2014. Given the inevitable legal challenges and regulatory inertia that accompany any proposed rule of this type, the full effects will not likely be felt until 2016 or later. Thus, the president has once again written another IOU to be deferred to another generation that will face the Hobsonian choice of paying the bill or rejecting the consensus Obama has invoked.

INDUSTRIAL-BOILER RULES

With the shadow of the massive Deepwater Horizon oil spill in the Gulf of Mexico still hanging over America, the EPA has used that tragedy to justify regulations that have nothing to do with petroleum exploration. An oil spill apparently excuses every bureaucratic excess that progressives can imagine. Scores of sources—from the boilers that provide heat to college campuses to the boilers that power ethanol plants, paper mills, and food-processing plants—will find it impossible to comply with new industrial-boiler regulations that the EPA proposed in 2010. Further, these regulations will give bureaucrats unprecedented authority to decide how these industries are run.

The rules in question are supposed to set new limits on emissions of potentially toxic materials from power plants. The regulation is generically known as "Boiler MACT" (Maximum Achievable Control Technology). However, what USEPA Administrator Lisa Jackson has proposed goes well beyond the realm of toxins; the agency is attempting to use these rules as a covert way of regulating greenhouse gases and giving big government a role in making operational decisions.

As noted previously, when the Clean Air Act first passed in 1970, the EPA was directed to develop rules to limit potentially toxic emissions, based solely on risk. That is, if the agency determined that a particular compound was being emitted in quantities sufficient to present an actual health hazard, then the EPA should develop rules to limit emissions of that compound. Using this approach, the EPA developed rules to limit emissions of seven potentially toxic materials. This upset environmental groups, which accused the EPA of shirking its responsibilities. That allegation was not true; the agency simply could not find significant risk anywhere else, but no matter: the enviromentalists demanded change, and change they got.

When the Clean Air Act was amended in 1990, the EPA was directed to limit emissions of 188 potentially toxic materials, using a technology-based approach. Very little actual science went into selecting those 188 (now 187) compounds, but the list made the Sierra Club and similar groups happy, and that was all that mattered. Under the new approach, the agency was directed to evaluate how industries were controlling toxins, to determine the top 12 percent doing the best job, and to use these top 12 percent to set the standard for each compound. Thus, the philosophical question behind controlling potentially toxic air pollutants shifted from "what *should* we do?" to "what *can* we do?" The EPA calls this approach "MACT." Scores of industries have their own MACT, outlining the way each is supposed to control potentially toxic materials and setting numerical emissions standards.

Boiler MACT, covering the industrial sector, was first proposed in 2003 under the Bush administration. The Sierra Club challenged it in court, and the EPA was directed to rewrite it. The problem that the Sierra Club had with Boiler MACT did not so much involve substance as it did style. The Sierra Club was not happy with the form of the regulation, or how the universe of regulated sources was defined. No surprise there: George W. Bush's EPA could have proposed shutting down every coal-fired power plant in the United States and the Sierra Club would still have said that he didn't go far enough to protect the environment. That is always the green mantra when a member of the GOP occupies the White House. Nonetheless, everyone expected that the *new* version of Boiler MACT would look a lot like the old one, but with more data to back it up, more justification with regard to affected sources, and reformatted language (though still impossible for an average Joe to understand). Until recently, that is what EPA staffers led the regulated community to expect.

However, Jackson's EPA proposed something quite different and disturbing. It effectively abandoned the "top 12 percent" formula, choosing instead to use laboratory detection limits to set limits in many cases. In other words, under the EPA's proposal, many potentially toxic pollutants will have to be controlled so tightly that no one will be able to find them. That is one step removed from setting emissions limits at zero, and just about as unrealistic and unachievable a goal.

The proposal also requires industrial-boiler operators to implement a government-approved energy-management program. The program will contain multiple elements. Operators will have to review architectural and engineering plans and the facility's operations and maintenance procedures. They will have to study fuel usage, energy-conservation measures, and ways to improve efficiency. After operators have done all of that, they will have to submit a report to the government that details their findings, including the cost of making specific improvement and the benefits of doing so. Government will thus be directly involved in approving operational and investment decisions in the manufacturing sector.

One can argue, and Lisa Jackson's EPA surely will, that getting the government involved in energy efficiency—that is, how boilers actually run—can affect the amount of potentially toxic emissions a facility puts out. However, that argument is very thin, especially when the rule in question already contains draconian limits. Energy-efficiency requirements are rather a backhand way of achieving the Obama administration's goal of reducing greenhouse-gas emissions, without having to go through the tiresome process of addressing "climate change" directly. Further, note that we are talking only about industrial boilers here. The EPA has recently released draft MACT rules that will affect the big, electricity-producing utility boilers that are far more significant in terms of size and greenhouse-gas emissions than those in the industrial sector. Can there be any question that this radical, extremist EPA will ask the power industry to accept equally unachievable limits and submit to even more big-government control? As far as this administration and progressives are concerned, the disaster in the Gulf is justification enough for every excess that big government can dream up.

ATTACKING DOMESTIC NATURAL-GAS PRODUCTION

In an economy full of problems, there are still a few high points. One of them, as you may have noticed if you pay attention to your utility bills, is that natural-gas prices are relatively low. Back in mid-2008, natural-gas prices hit record highs. The market reacted as it is supposed to: exploration took off, production increased, and now, almost two years later, the cost of natural gas has stabilized at a comfortable level, amid normal seasonal variations. We should not have to worry about this sector of the economy, but a dark cloud looms on the horizon in the form of yet another environmental initiative that the Obama administration is pushing forward, one that has the potential to cut domestic natural-gas production, cost us jobs and revenue, and force energy prices upward.

There is quite a bit of natural gas and oil trapped in shale and rock formations located thousands of feet underground. The tried-and-true technique of hydraulic-fracturing has been used for about sixty years to coax these hydrocarbons to deep wells, where they can be recovered. In simple terms, hydraulic-fracturing fluids are pumped down into a deep well under pressure. The fluid consists mostly of water and sand, with a small amount of other chemicals. As the pressurized fluid is distributed along a horizontal plane, it creates microfractures in the rock holding the natural gas. The sand particles hold these fractures open, allowing gas to flow along the path of least resistance up into the borehole of the well.

More than a million natural-gas wells utilize hydraulic fracturing in the United States. About 95 percent of natural-gas wells in the country use this form, or an analogous form, of reservoir enhancement to recover energy. The process is an important—some would say vital—piece of the puzzle if the nation is going to maintain some degree of energy independence. However, the technology caught the attention of Barack Obama's EPA, which set about "studying the issue." Uttered by members of this administration, those three words generally sound rather ominous. This was no exception. "Studying the issue," whatever the issue, typically means more regulations, more restrictions, and higher costs. When it comes to a part of our economy as vital as the energy sector, one has to ask, How many more studies and subsequent "recommendations" can we afford?

Why is the EPA studying hydraulic fracturing? For environmental reasons, of course. Scattered, unconfirmed, and wholly anecdotal claims that hydraulic fracturing has contaminated drinking water in a few locations across the nation spurred the EPA into action. From a scientific point of view, why the EPA would lend any credibility to these tales is hard to understand. Nor is it clear why the EPA would allocate $1.9 million dollars to take another look at a technology that has been studied excessively, not only by the oil and natural-gas industries, but by the EPA itself. A 2004 EPA study concluded that hydraulic fracturing did not present any threat to human health and the environment, but, of course, that was George W. Bush's EPA. Any of its decisions are subject to Barack Obama's reconsideration.

For a number of reasons, spending almost two million dollars to reconfirm what we already know is just plain silly. Chemically, as noted above, hydraulic-fracturing fluid is overwhelmingly water and sand (or ceramic, or some other inert solid used to keep rock pores open). Other chemicals, which are often proprietary, represent a very small fraction of the whole. Geologically, the formations holding the gas and oil are located thousands of feet underground, under layers of different strata, while drinking water aquifers are typically no more than a few hundred feet below ground. The natural gas recovered, like the fracturing fluid, will naturally follow the path of least resistance and flow to the borehole that's been drilled for that purpose, rather than find a tortuous path through all the surrounding layers of rock and sediment. Furthermore, consider this: even as the EPA looks at ways to restrict an important means of producing energy, it is simultaneously developing regulations that encourage another segment of the power industry to inject chemicals deep underground without the kind of relief valve that a borehole provides. Carbon storage and sequestration is the leading, EPA-approved way to reduce carbon dioxide emissions from coal-fired power plants. In this case, carbon dioxide is injected deep underground at high pressures, but because there is no well to relieve the pressure, it is free to find fractures that will carry it, and any contaminants from the stack gas that remain, into aquifers.

The Environmental Engineering Committee (EEC) of EPA's Science Advisory Board is in charge of studying hydraulic fracturing. The EEC has sixteen members: fourteen academics and two consultants. Not a single industry expert sits on the committee. The energy industry will be free to comment on the committee's work, of course, but is Obama's EPA likely to pay serious attention to experts who represent evil corporate interests?

According to a study conducted by IHS Global Insight, a ban on hydraulic fracturing would cost the United States $374 billion in lost gross domestic product (GDP) by 2014, would result in the loss of about 3 million jobs, and would require a 60 percent increase in imported oil and natural gas to make up the difference. Placing restrictions on the fluids that can be used for hydraulic fracturing would be slightly less painful, but painful enough. In that scenario, IHS's study foresees a $172 billion reduction in GDP, 1.4 million jobs lost, and a 30 percent increase in energy imports.

It should be noted that hydraulic fracturing is already regulated on the state and federal levels. Studying the practice once again will lead to one of two results. Either the EPA will conclude that existing regulatory protections are sufficient, which does not seem likely given this administration's record when it comes to environmental issues, or the EPA will deem it necessary to pile another layer of crippling regulations onto an industry that has been one of the few bright spots in a floundering economy.

NEW STORMWATER RULES

National unemployment rates may be high, but there is no shortage of work if one happens to be an academic willing to conduct EPA-funded research and undertake EPA-directed studies. Last October, USEPA formally began the process of creating new stormwater management rules. We have actually got quite a pile of stormwater management rules already, including measures crafted during the Clinton administration and then implemented during the Bush administration. However, having never met a regulatory program that went far enough for her tastes, EPA administrator Lisa Jackson took one look at a report prepared by the National Research Council (NRC) that reviewed the Agency's stormwater management programs and fell in love. This will come as a shock, but the NRC committee that looked into the issue—a committee consisting mostly of academics—concluded that new stormwater regulations are desperately needed.

The NRC's recommendations are troubling but entirely typical of what happens when a group of professors get together to decide how to run the world. It should be noted up front that I did not read the NRC's report in full, as the organization charges the public more than forty dollars to purchase copies of this study, notwithstanding that it is being used to set public policy. No doubt the full report contains a number of hidden gems, but the Executive Summary, which NRC kindly allows citizens to download for free, provides enough of a peek behind the curtains. If Jackson's EPA follows the NRC's advice—and history suggests that Jackson generally takes the most radical environmental advice available—then more rules are coming, more restrictions on your lives, and, of course, more tax dollars that need to be redistributed. If one thinks that using the adjective "radical" to describe the advice Jackson is getting from NRC is a bit over the top, there's no need to take my word for it. Here is how NRC describes what is needed in their Executive Summary: "Radical changes to the current regulatory program (see Chapter 6) appear necessary to provide meaningful regulation of stormwater dischargers in the future."

What kind of radical changes appear necessary? How about having USEPA use its licensing authority to place further restrictions on the formulation and use of even more consumer products? Quoting again from the Executive Summary:

> EPA should engage in much more vigilant regulatory oversight in the national licensing of products that contribute significantly to stormwater pollution. De-icing chemicals, materials used in brake linings, motor fuels, asphalt sealants, fertilizers, and a variety of other products should be examined for their potential contamination of stormwater. Currently, EPA does not apparently utilize its existing licensing authority to regulate these products in a way that minimizes their contribution to stormwater contamination. States can also enact restrictions on or tax the application of pesticides or other particularly toxic products. Even local efforts could ultimately help motivate broader scale, federal restrictions on particular products.

In other words, if a product is used outdoors or is part of a machine that is used outdoors—your automobile, for example— it needs to be regulated, restricted, and possibly taxed. Just what an ailing economy needs! What could possibly go wrong? It is easy to imagine some well-meaning EPA committee deciding that tire residue left on the street, to take one example, helps deteriorate stormwater quality. Ergo, the EPA should come up with standards for tire wear. Of course, such standards might make tires more expensive, but expense is not the EPA's problem; it is here to save a planet or two. Or perhaps such standards would unintentionally lead to more blowouts, but that will be the tire manufacturer's fault, not the EPA's. Of course, we do not know if any of this is going to happen as far as tires are concerned, but that kind of thing will inevitably happen somewhere when EPA interferes with the free market. It always does. The EPA is Exhibit A when it comes to demonstrating the timeless truth that is the Law of Unintended Consequences.

NRC also believes that another layer of bureaucracy is necessary to better manage stormwater. They believe that stormwater permitting should be "watershed based," a proposal that would essentially create a new regulatory authority in between the local agencies that already have jurisdiction over stormwater and state and federal agencies charged with overseeing their programs. How will we pay for more rules and more bureaucracy? The federal government ought to pour more money into these programs, of course.

The regulated community is not quite as fired up about NRC's recommendations as Lisa Jackson is. Many members of the regulated community recently commented most unfavorably about these proposals. Their comments are part of the USEPA docket covering a proposal to start gathering information in anticipation of formulating new rules. Ironically, the regulated community that has offered damning comments in this case does not consist of evil corporations: rather, it is made up of the organizations that are currently responsible for stormwater management, which, like the EPA itself, are units of government. The question of whether one regulatory agency can regulate to the point of offending fellow regulators has now been answered in the affirmative. The National Association of Flood and Stormwater Management Agencies (NAFSMA) commented on EPA's proposed Information Collection Request (ICR), wondering, among other things, why EPA was abandoning the Phase I and Phase II stormwater-management practices that have been put into place already. From NAFSMA's comments, dated December 23, 2009:

> In addition to our comments on the specific elements of the ICR, NAFSMA must express its strong concern that EPA's announced intention to promulgate a substantial change to the Phase I and Phase II stormwater program, based on this ICR, constitutes a breach of the current regulations and the program evaluation agreement reached through the Stormwater Phase II

Federal Advisory Council Act (FACA) in which NAFSMA was
an active and involved participant with three of our members
involved throughout the process.

This statement comes from an organization representing
almost one hundred state and local stormwater-management agencies, serving about 76 million people. Many comments in the docket
from individual agencies themselves are similarly critical, of both the
specifics of the proposed regulations and of the way that the EPA is
trying to extend its reach. I cannot recall the last time local environmental agencies were this critical of their federal counterpart. While
no friend of industry, the EPA has traditionally blunted most of the
worst excesses that extreme environmental groups would otherwise
foist on America. No longer. Little distinguishes Greenpeace and
Lisa Jackson's EPA.

When pressed, one can usually get an honest, informed environmental advocate to admit that our air and water actually become
cleaner under George W. Bush's administration, as they have under
every administration since Nixon's. The problem (such as it is), they
say, is that Bush did not go far enough. That's a political argument,
not a scientific one, because no Republican president can ever go far
enough to satisfy the environmental movement. Bush's EPA set regulations reducing mercury emissions from power plants on a massive scale. It was not enough. Bush's EPA faithfully followed George
H. W. Bush's wetlands-restoration policies, such that we had many
more wetlands when George W. Bush left office than when he first
took the oath of office. It was not enough. Most veterans in the EPA
understand the politics involved and take that kind of criticism with
more than a few grains of salt. Lisa Jackson appears to have swallowed the most extreme environmental-activist arguments whole
and, mostly unnoticed by both the press and policymakers, has
unleashed a series of crippling initiatives that will do untold damage
to the nation's economy at a time when we can least afford it.

CHAPTER THIRTEEN

FIXING THE SYSTEM

THE SYSTEM, WE HAVE CONCLUDED, DAMAGES business and, too often, is counterproductive to the environment. How can we fix it? Let us start to answer that question by considering the ways that the current system is most deficient. Several themes run through this analysis of the current system of environmental regulation.

1. COST-EFFECTIVENESS

Environmental regulations are supposed to consider cost-effectiveness, and in a way, they do. However, the costs actually considered are severely limited. An economic analysis of a particular regulation considers the capital cost of new equipment, the operating and maintenance costs of that equipment, and the labor costs associated with compliance. What the analysis does not consider is the cost to the business in time required to achieve compliance with a new rule, which may involve waiting for new permits, finding the people to implement the rule, and just figuring out what in the heck all the legalese means.

Many new rules cause problems because they are simply too complex. As we have seen, responsible companies who want to do nothing more than comply and be good neighbors can be ensnared in regulatory traps. Having complied with regulations A, B, and C, they are completely unprepared to face the possibility of regulation D. When that inevitably trips them up, cynicism takes over. If there is no way to figure out the system, why bother? When it comes to expanding operations, they look to another state—or another country—where life is simpler.

2. EQUITY

From an American manufacturer's point of view, the agency's penalty policy ranks just behind the O.J. trial in terms of injustice. Penalties are calculated on the basis of supposed economic benefit, but the definition of economic benefit is ridiculously broad. When a manufacturer or small-time real-estate investor can be fined for hundreds of thousands because he did not file the correct piece of paper at the right time, something is very wrong with the system. The current policy does not effectively distinguish between cases where there is no environmental harm and those where there is some degree of harm. Not only does that hurt the pocketbook of the employers who pay the fines; it also creates an atmosphere in which responsible entrepreneurs are less likely to take the risks that keep the economy healthy. Why bother to do the right thing when the government cannot wait to trip you up on a technicality?

3. REPETITION

It is not unusual for an American manufacturer to submit the same information in many different formats. Between emission reports,

Form R, Tier II, wastewater reports, and hazardous-waste reports, a company may generate the same information—in part or in whole—over and over. The way that information is presented changes from form to form, although the basic data does not. Worse, some nuance in a single report may change—with a particular chemical being added or subtracted from a list, for example—unbeknownst to the company that is writing the report. "Didn't I just submit this information?" a frustrated manufacturer will ask. He probably did, but it does not matter. Once is not enough.

4. EMOTION

Finally, it must be recognized that emotion takes precedence over science whenever a particular project attracts popular attention. As a public body, ultimately dependent on public funds, the EPA—both nationally and on the state level—responds to emotion. That response can be devastating to the companies involved.

A big part of that problem is that there is not any recognizable, truly scientific process available for review. Superficially, technical review is supposed to take precedence. In reality, the process works only in those cases where there is no public outcry. Should the local populace become aroused, no matter how ridiculous the basis of people's objections, the standards will change. The net result is environmental injustice, although not in the terms that environmental groups typically espouse. When clamor, rather than science, is the decisive determinant, prudence takes a back seat to noise.

An affluent neighborhood or town may successfully make enough noise to oppose a local power station that would pollute less than a bigger power plant down the road, at the cost of increasingly unreliable electrical supply. At the same time, a less affluent town may pay no attention to a similar project, and thereby secure the electricity it needs for a long time to come—so long as the project does not attract the attention of powerful, national environmental groups. All things being equal, poorer communities that are able to proceed unnoticed are generally the beneficiaries of new industrial projects more often than their richer cousins. Is that a bad thing? No, but neither is this practice the environmental injustice that environmental groups so often decry. It is a reflection of what communities value most: prosperity or fear, which is an awfully poor way to make decisions.

Fixing these problems requires a sober evaluation of the obstacles that stand in the way. There are more than a few. Among those are:

1. PERCEPTION

More environmental regulation is needed, from much of the public's point of view, because the environment is being destroyed. That is simply not true, but it provides ample justification for every rule—no matter how unnecessary or intrusive—that is promulgated.

2. IT TAKES A FOREST

With controls already in place throughout most of the industrial sector that needed controls, the EPA's objective shifted in the mid-1990s from reducing pollution to ensuring that controls were being properly and consistently operated. So far so good. But the agency's preferred method of monitoring compliance has been to require more paper: more reports, more records, and more notifications. The public is largely unaware of the extent of the compliance burden and accepts the EPA's contention that a forest of trees is necessary to maintain environmental progress.

3. THE FEAR INDUSTRY

The multibillion-dollar environmental industry has a tremendous investment in maintaining the illusion that the planet is dying. The next time an environmental group admits that progress is being made will be the first. Fear equals funding in their business, and any time someone tries to reform the clunky regulatory system, environmental lobbyists will equate "regulatory reform" to "environmental backsliding."

4. OPPORTUNISM MEETS INDIFFERENCE

Both political parties are obstacles to reform. Democrats are an obstacle because their natural constituency expects an anti-industry posture from the party. Most Republicans, on the other hand, see the environment as a throwaway issue. It is awfully complex and ultimately not worth the effort, in the view of many Republican politicians. Indeed, as we have seen, many of the most significant environmental statutes were championed by the GOP.

Quite frankly, such obstacles are probably insurmountable. Overcoming them requires a massive education campaign that will leave members of the public largely indifferent unless and until it is absolutely clear that their own pocketbooks are threatened. Who wants to learn any more science than is absolutely necessary? The public-relations issue is a windmill that is beyond the scope or expertise of this particular Cervantes fan. Let us make a leap of extreme faith, however. Let us imagine a country that understood the need to reform environmental regulation and was willing to adopt sensible reform. What would environmental regulation look like in Utopia? What follows are the steps needed to fix each of the systemic problems that we have identified:

1. COST-EFFECTIVENESS

As we have seen, a few large categories of sources account for the vast majority of emissions in every form. In the case of air pollution, it is large, fossil-fired power plants and vehicles that are—by far—most important. Big municipal, agricultural, and industrial sources account for most water pollution. The regulatory effort does not, unfortunately, reflect the same priorities.

The same sorts of rules apply, generally speaking, to a source that emits 25 tons of air pollution as one that emits 2,500 tons, so regulators apply nearly the same level of command and control to both. This does not mean that large sources are underregulated. It means that smaller sources—those that have little effect on the environment—are overregulated. The EPA spends too much time and money closely watching sources that do not really matter in the big picture. The little stakeholders spend too much time and money trying to keep up with a structure designed for the big stakeholders.

Fixing the system should, therefore, start with the rules. Smaller sources should not have to face an ever-growing set of reporting, record-keeping, and certification requirements, particularly if they are employing state-of-the-art control devices in the first place. The EPA would argue that the current set of rules fulfill that objective. They do not. Today's environmental regulations intrude into the office of the plant manager, the engineer designing a new product, and every salesperson looking for a new market. A system based only on emissions would focus on the two issues that are ultimately relevant to small-source compliance: (1) production- or material-use records, which can be easily maintained by a given company, and (2) annual process inspections by state engineers to ensure that each control system is working properly.

Material and product changes within that system should be freely allowed, without going through the lengthy and costly permit-modification process. Will such a relaxation of accountability result in the occasional mistake or excess? Of course. But so what? Small sources do not matter, remember? Keep the system as tight as it is now for the big compnaies and there is no chance that today's brightening environmental picture will dim. In fact, by greatly relieving the pressure on the companies that employ state-of-the-art controls, quite the opposite will happen. When plant managers understand that they can achieve more freedom of action by doing the best they possibly can, they will want to do nothing less.

2. EQUITY

Today's enforcement climate is an enormous disincentive to the entrepreneur. Confronted by a system he cannot understand, with unknown traps waiting just ahead to cost him his investment, savvy businessmen are increasingly reluctant to start or expand manufacturing operations in this country. Under USEPA's penalty policy, actual environmental harm is a minor component in a penalty calculation. Economic benefit, which is, as we have seen, a very tenuous idea, is the controlling factor. This set of priorities needs to change before we kill the goose that lays the golden egg.

A company that is late in filing its Form R (Toxic Release Inventory) report, even though it has been in compliance with all emissions limits, should not face tens or hundreds of thousands of dollars in fines, for the same reason that the IRS does not assess a penalty against a person who overpaid their taxes but filed a late return. If no harm, why call a foul?

Environmental groups will cry foul, of course. Any relaxation in the penalty policy, even where the penalty policy makes no sense, will translate into a planet-endangering relaxation. That is silly. A penalty policy that focuses on actual environmental harm—instead of perceived economic benefit—may cut into the EPA's budget, but it will not have any discernable effect on pollution. Not to worry about those revenue reductions, for we have reduced the costs in step one, remember? With a more reasonable level of attention paid to the sources that have little effect on the environment, the federal and state EPAs will not need as much cash in the first place.

Requirements for permitting small emitters need to be vastly simplified as well, if for no other reason than to help them compete in a global marketplace.

As the system works today, no one can make a change to their plant that affects pollutant output without a lengthy review process, unless they fall into a relatively small exemption list in their home state. Exemption lists need to be expanded, replacement-in-kind projects should be given a free pass, and permit review for low-impact projects should be expedited.

One big advantage that American businesses ought to have in the world market is mobility—the ability to respond quickly to changing market conditions. Our financial-sales and durable-goods-supply infrastructures are designed to be ultraresponsive. However, our environmental regulatory structure is designed to bring projects to a screeching halt. Expedited review for projects with low-impact potential makes sense for everyone. Let business move with the marketplace and catch up on the details as they proceed.

3. REPETITION

This recommendation is ridiculously easy. In this electronic age, nothing could be easier than implementing a single, consolidated, environmental-reporting system to replace the mishmash of multiple reports required under the overlapping statutes and regulations in force today. Rather than endlessly recrunching the same numbers for Form R, Tier II, RCRA, TSCA, the Clean Air Act, and Clean Water Act, why not submit one set of numbers each year?

There are a limited set of factors that determine how much and into what media a source releases environmental pollution. Raw-material use, fuel use, production rate, control-device efficiency, and media-specific (air, water, ground) release rates define the picture across the board. Why not submit a single annual report that covers all bases? Form R–The Toxic Release Inventory—comes closest to achieving the objective of all of today's systems. However, Form R is limited. It applies only to those materials used in a certain threshold quantity—typically 10,000 pounds per year. Why not expand that system, by lowering the threshold, and close all the loops with one blow?

The effect of such a change on small to midsize manufacturers would be electric, with no discernable environmental downside. If businesses knew they had a single, simple reporting method, much of their fear of the system would evaporate.

Proactive monitoring, in the communications age, should also be available for any business that might wish to utilize it. As it stands today, the regulatory system calls for companies to self-monitor their processes, self-identify deviations, and self-report any problems. Not surprisingly, companies—especially smaller concerns without a dedicated environmental staff—can sometimes be remiss in fulfilling those obligations. Let us say a company uses a thermal oxidizer to control its solvent emissions. The rule says that the oxidizer must operate at 1400 degrees Fahrenheit or more to destroy the pollutant.

The company records the oxidizer temperature on a strip-chart recorder. If there is a problem, if the temperature dips below 1400 degrees Farenheit, the company is supposed to identify and report it. Sometimes, companies are late to do so and are penalized as a result. This failure is not because they do not care, but because they are paying attention to other things, like production and keeping the company solvent.

Why not relieve such a company of this burden, especially if it is not very good at managing it? Let the data-recording system report directly to the EPA, where an alarm is triggered if the magic number is not met? With current technology, that sort of system is not only achievable, it would be a lot cheaper than sending people out to each facility to pore over mountains of records. Automated monitoring is available for more and more pollutant streams. Such a system would be strictly voluntary—a company could choose automated monitoring or the traditional method—and assume the cost in either case.

Automated monitoring would also be a boom to the environment, assuming that the EPA was directed to manage the system in a reasonable fashion. As a benefit for entering the system, companies should receive a waiver when they respond appropriately. In our example, the facility operator would get a call from the EPA, informing him that he appears to have a control problem. The operator would then have a preset amount of time (three hours?) to fix the problem, show that the reading was erroneous, or shut down the process. As long as the company meets one of these criteria, it would not be subject to penalties.

4. EMOTION

Emotion can best be diffused at the local level. The problem with communities evaluating projects on an individual basis is that they do so without any sense of context. When a company proposes a new facility or expanded operations, it is too late for education. Emotionally driven activists and towns people, whipped into a frenzy by environmental groups and the mainstream media, are certain that ecological doom is just around the corner. If one believes that he is tottering on the edge of death and destruction, every molecule of pollution—no matter how insignificant—will grow to mammoth proportions.

Individual communities, on the municipal and county level, should establish their own environmental standards. That may seem to run counter to the theme of this book, but local government is not the problem—big government is. The feds can ignore economic growth because they operate in an environment where fiscal resources are limited only by political will, not commercial or industrial health. Municipalities and counties have to consider factors such as employment and the tax base that do not play into the federal equation.

So let us adopt a two-part plan at the local level. First, let the municipalities and counties establish an environmental baseline for their communities. This document would provide a record of ecological quality within their jurisdiction, in terms of pollutants emitted, pollution exposure, and environmentally sensitive areas. It should examine those factors in the context of state and federal standards and in terms of health effects. Having established a baseline, and therefore a basis for comparison, towns could then consider where they want to go. Since most community objections involve issues that go beyond federal and state guidelines, should there not be a set of local guidelines in place that would create a meaningful context?

It is one thing for a community activist to object to a project because it will add 2 parts per million of solids to regional wastewater discharge into a local stream that is already 100 parts per million below clean-water standards. The feds and state can say it is OK, but if these 2 parts per million translate into 200 tons of extra pollution per year, the municipality will be hard-pressed to defend the move. Numbers are scary, unless, of course, one develops the ability to judge the numbers beforehand. With environmental factors calculated into a local growth-with-conservation plan, a municipality or county can point to a reasonable local plan and say: "Yes, this is OK. It fits in with a responsible plan of growth for our community."

The fact is that local environmental response does play, and will continue to play, a significant role in commercial and industrial growth. If municipalities are to manage such growth reasonably, rather than responding to the loudest voice—however unreasonable—a standard should be established that provides a reasonable basis for future decisions. Given a poorly educated public in an increasingly complex world, the only hope to combat the Chicken Littles is to preemptively decide what is and is not acceptable. Local standards and guidelines will give local government the freedom to do what they know is right, without fear of electoral retribution. They will have a document and date to point to, and they can say, "We're meeting our plan."

One other important issue about reform needs to be considered: a more liberal regulatory environment would result in more large, capital-intensive projects. For the EPA as well as for the American economy, that is where the real money is. If a company plans a $100 million expansion, a couple hundred thousand in permit fees are baseline noise. If the rules were reformed to allow multibillion-dollar construction of a new oil refinery in the United States (which has not happened since the 1970s), an enlightened EPA could tap into a gold mine. The big money, for everyone, is with big capital projects. From a wholly self-interested point of view, regulators should strive to create an environment where such projects are desirable. Fining companies struggling to compete is killing the goose. Encouraging responsible growth is harvesting the golden eggs.

Unfortunately, none of this is likely to happen. Not today. Not tomorrow. Not for ten years. Environmental regulation will grow and grow, unchecked, for a long time to come. It is a silent killer, a cancer slowly eating away at the most productive parts of society. Perhaps someday, when China, India, and Taiwan have stripped every last manufacturing job from the United States, we may realize that we have been a bit too idealistic. That will not happen anytime soon. We can only hope that it does not happen too late.

But it probably will.

RECENT DEVELOPMENTS

AS THIS BOOK IS BEING PREPARED TO GO TO PRESS, a bit of pushback has been directed against the EPA and its aggressive, anti-industry policies. Republicans and Democrats settled on a budget in April that included a $1.6 billion reduction in the EPA budget. Earlier in the year, the Senate came within one vote of passing a bill that would have prohibited the EPA from regulating greenhouse gases without specific congressional approval. Prospective presidential candidate Newt Gingrich publicly suggested that it might be time to do away with the EPA and replace it with another organization that is more in tune with America's economic realities.

All of these efforts are welcome. However, while they might represent an ebbing of the green tide, one should not be fooled into believing that we are witnessing a reversal of that tide. The EPA's budget needed to be cut, but Lisa Jackson's budget has been so grossly inflated during her tenure as administrator that a $1.6 billion reduction represents a step toward sanity, not sanity itself. Furthermore, lest we forget, the EPA has the ability to generate revenue itself through aggressive enforcement programs against industry. Possibly, all the $1.6 billion reduction has achieved is to stimulate some EPA lawyers into finding more supposed miscreants with deep pockets from whom they can extort multimillion-dollar settlements.

The move to get the EPA out of the greenhouse-gas-regulation business was a noble attempt, but it was doomed to failure even if the bill had passed the Senate. President Obama was sure to veto the measure, and the Senate never had enough votes to override that veto. Besides, as we have seen, even if the EPA were forced to stop regulating greenhouse gases directly through the Clean Air Act, the EPA has a plethora of indirect measures to reduce fossil-fuel use. Many state-level programs do the same thing. Dismantling greenhouse-gas regulation and taking advantage of our plentiful, cheap fossil-fuel resources would require a massive rollback across the board, not merely slapping Lisa Jackson's wrist for dipping into the wrong regulatory cookie jar.

Gingrich's call to tear down the EPA and replace it with a new agency makes all the sense in the world. However, how such a proposal could come to pass is hard to imagine, even if Republicans control both houses of Congress and the White House in 2013. The hyperbole and hysteria from the left would be deafening if such an attempt were made. One suspects that Gingrich understands that. The speaker remains one of the most brilliant minds in the political arena today, as well as a very savvy politician. Taking the extreme position effectively gives Gingrich maneuvering room should he make a White House run. If he cannot have the EPA replaced, he might be able to leverage that stance to see the agency reformed.

When one examines the current political and public climate regarding the EPA and needlessly aggressive environmental regulation, drawing even cautiously optimistic conclusions would be going too far. The green message is ingrained in our culture. So many companies have manipulated it to their own profitable advantage that it will take years, if not decades, to restore some sense of balance between environmental sanity and economic reality. Yet, as the proverb goes, the longest journey begins with a single step. Perhaps we are witnessing those first cautious steps today.

The essential question is how much risk we as a society are willing to assume in order to reap the benefits of the modern world. At one end of the spectrum are those people who believe that the modern world and technology are inherently evil. Unabomber Ted Kaczynski is the quintessential example of this philosophy. Ironically (and contrary to popular belief), Kaczynski did not oppose technology for environmental reasons. Instead, he believed that a technologically advanced society must necessarily infringe on individual freedoms. The environmental community's attitude toward technology is as paranoid as Kaczynski's, although (with the exception of eco-terrorist groups such as Earth First) it is a few steps shy of advocating unabomber-style violence.

Consider the way that environmental groups, politicians, and the media reacted when a devastating earthquake hit Japan on March 11, 2011. Thousands lost their lives in the wake of the fifth-biggest earthquake ever recorded and the subsequent tsunami. Tens of thousands more saw their homes destroyed and their lives shattered. It was a tragedy in many ways, but there was one tragedy that—incredibly—never happened. Nonetheless, this non-tragedy captured the world's attention in the days and weeks following the earthquake. Hysterical, wildly misleading stories filled the air, warning that reactors at the Fukushima nuclear complex were in danger of a catastrophic meltdown. American newspapers and bloggers speculated about the number of U.S. citizens who would inevitably be killed once the killer cloud of radioactive particles emanating from Fukushima drifted over American soil. Politicians and pundits solemnly declared that no new nuclear reactors would ever be built in America, just when it seemed that we had finally gotten over the previous non-disaster of Three Mile Island.

All of that hysteria is remarkable considering that nobody—not one person—died as a result of any of the fires, explosions, or controlled releases of radioactive material from the Fukushima reactors. Instead of poisoning the waters for new nuclear development, a dispassionate observer might be comforted by the fact that a plant designed more than thirty years ago rode out a magnitude 9.0 earthquake and survived intact. Given that everything that could go wrong did go wrong after the tsunami hit the plant, it's all the more remarkable that no one died as engineers and workers scrambled to stabilize the situation. However, we live in this Age of Fear. In the Age of Fear, few technologies are as feared as nuclear power, at least in America. The truth behind the Fukushima story and popular perception of it are very different. Retelling that story will be instructive as we consider where we are when it comes to restoring the balance between risks and rewards.

The engineers from General Electric and Tokyo Electric who designed the Fukushima reactors understood that the plant was being built in an earthquake zone. Good engineers (and engineers from GE and Japan are among the best in the world) always over-design critical components. In this case, the most critical components were the primary containment vessels in which the nuclear reaction powering the boiling water reactors took place. The vessels were designed to survive the worst earthquake imaginable, and on March 11, 2011, they did just that. No containment vessels ruptured, and no radioactive material was released as massive shock waves shook the plant.

The earthquake knocked out power to the plant, but that, too, had been planned for. Back-up diesel generators kicked in, ensuring that water would continue to flow into the reactors to keep the nuclear cores cool. What the engineers in the 1970s did not understand, or at least plan for, was that a massive earthquake could generate a massive tsunami. The 30-foot wall of water that battered Japan's coastline flooded the Fukushima complex, taking out the back-up generators, cutting off the flow of fresh water to the active reactors.

Operators moved to start shutting down the reactors, but that process takes time and cooling water is needed to keep core temperatures down while the nuclear reactions in fuel rods slow to a stop.

Tokyo Electric understood that seawater could be used to cool the cores, but seawater is very corrosive and would damage many reactor components beyond repair. So using seawater would basically be an admission that the reactors—a multibillion dollar investment— would never run again. Right or wrong, Tokyo Electric decided not to use seawater immediately to cool the reactors.

As they tried to shut down the reactors, core temperatures rose high enough to split water into its elemental component parts: hydrogen and oxygen. As anyone who has seen vintage video of the *Hindenburg* disaster can attest, hydrogen and water can recombine with violently spectacular results if someone provides a spark. This happened at Fukushima. Hydrogen explosions destroyed secondary containment structures on a couple of reactors. Primary containment structures remained intact. Losing secondary containment was an annoyance, but the event did not have any practical damaging effects.

Tokyo Electric then decided that it was prudent to use seawater to cool at-risk reactors. That decision did not completely solve the problem, but it helped the company better manage the crisis. Shutting down the damaged reactors was a balancing act. The primary containment vessels could contain a certain amount of pressure as cooling water boiled off, but the vessels could not contain an infinite amount of pressure. At times, Tokyo Electric had to vent off some of the gases in the vessel to relieve the pressure. While these gases were radioactive, they hardly represented anything near the degree of risk that the technologically challenged mainstream media would have had us believe. Because it was extremely short-lived, the vast majority of the radioactivity represented no threat to human health or the environment. Furthermore, there was not enough of the remaining—potentially troublesome—kinds of radioactivity to worry about.

Radioactive water from one reactor appears to have leaked out to some extent, although reports are still sketchy as of this writing. As a precautionary measure, Tokyo Electric collected the water and disposed of it at sea, far from any human habitation. The sea naturally contains radioactive compounds, as does the soil. The additional amount of radioactivity introduced by Tokyo Electric will be baseline noise compared to the natural background.

If the public and the politicians and the pundits truly understood the lessons of Fukushima, they would rally behind nuclear power as never before. The nuclear-power technology we have today is orders of magnitude safer than we had access to forty years ago. Other than the Pacific coast and the New Madrid, Missouri, area, no place in the United States exhibits anything close to the geological instability that one finds in Japan. If a 40-year-old plant half a world away can survive a 9.0 and not kill anyone, is that not all the proof we need that nuclear power is a safe, beneficial technology?

But perhaps the assumed stigma of nuclear power in the modern world is not the best example to use if we are to illustrate the true, hypersensitive nature of the Age of Fear. Let us consider the growing rift within the environmental community itself. The battle is between those environmental advocates who fervently believe that any sort of combustion process puts lives at risk and the environmental advocates who recognize that releasing energy through combustion is a necessary—and desirable—part of life, so long as combustion does not involve fossil fuels. Increasing evidence suggests that this issue will cause a civil war of sorts among the green crowd.

At the center of the controversy, we find a seemingly innocuous concept that has been around for hundreds of thousands of years: burning natural materials such as wood and other plants to release useful energy. To put it another way, the environmental community is divided over the subject of fire. While environmental groups march in lockstep in their core belief that burning fossil fuels such as coal and oil is inherently evil, most mainstream environmental organizations, the Sierra Club and Natural Resources Defense Council, for example, support biomass combustion. The term "biomass" is a catchall that covers a range of fuels from wood to ethanol to dedicated grasses to the gases created as garbage decays in a landfill.

Burning biomass is acceptable to most mainstream environmental groups because doing so does not release additional carbon into the environment. The carbon contained in wood, for example, originated in the atmosphere. Thus, when you burn wood and re-release that carbon, you are simply returning the carbon that was formerly in the atmosphere back from where it came. It is kind of the ultimate carbon-recycling program.

Environmental groups contrast the natural carbon contained in biomass from the sequestered carbon contained in fossil fuels. The carbon contained in coal has not been part of the carbon cycle that includes atmospheric dispersion for many millions of years. Rather, it has been sitting underground, stored—sequestered—and thus not contributing to the growth of plants and crops. It is this extra carbon released whenever we burn coal, oil, or gas that has environmental groups in a tizzy.

Primarily, they hate fossil fuels because they cling to the idea that we are at a tipping point when it comes to global warming and the concentration of greenhouse gases in the atmosphere. However, environmental groups have also attacked fossil fuels for reasons that have nothing to do with global warming. They have used every excuse they can think of to attack coal combustion. Burning coal, they tell us, creates tiny particulates that can get into our lungs, causing respiratory problems and death. Coal combustion leads to the formation of nitrogen oxides, which react to form ground-level ozone, which in turn creates problems for asthmatics. By-products of coal combustion include highly toxic compounds known to cause cancer.

In truth, these flanking attacks against coal had very little merit. As we have seen, America has made tremendous strides in reducing emissions and cleaning up our air. Industry plays a smaller and smaller role in generating air pollutants of all kinds as time goes on. The secondary risks of producing tiny particulates, ozone, and toxic pollutants from power plants have grown so small that it is incredible that anyone would ever bother to worry about them. Consider, for example, that the greatest exposure to fine-particulate matter and toxic pollutants that the average American will face involves standing over a charcoal grill or sitting around a campfire. Both of those common activities release high concentrations of fine particulates and partially burned toxic pollutants directly into the breathing zone of the people standing near the source of combustion. Neither situation should be worrisome.

Nonetheless, in their desperation to demonize coal combustion, environmental groups such as the Sierra Club ignore the natural sources and everyday situations that would generate the common air pollutants they prefer to describe in deadly terms. Today, we are led by an administration that wholly signs on to the idea that the continued combustion of fossil fuels will cause catastrophic climate change. Still, the Obama administration has enough technically savvy professionals to understand that the "zero-emissions" technologies of wind power and solar energy can never come close to replacing the power generated through fossil-fuel combustion. If we put nuclear energy aside for a moment (though we should not), the only viable, reliable alternative to fossil-fuel combustion is biomass combustion. Think of the issue this way: if we are not allowed to recover energy from the carbon that has been lying around underground, then the next best alternative is to grow our own carbon-containing fuels to burn.

What about those secondary issues? Do they disappear when we burn biomass? Fine particulates, nitrogen oxides, and toxic air pollutants are created when one burns anything. The important consideration is how much of each is released and how much of each a person might be exposed to. Those factors have very little to do with the fuel being combusted. Individual exposure to air pollutants involves carefully considering a number of technical issues. For instance, the more completely a fuel is burned, the less air pollutants are created. Control devices, like bag filters and scrubbers, will markedly reduce emissions. The taller the smokestack, the more the pollutants coming out of that smokestack are dispersed, which reduces exposure. With the possible—and dubious—exception of the carbon distinction we might make between fossil fuels and biomass fuels, nothing distinguishes the two. In terms of all pollutants except greenhouse gases, all fuels are basically created equal.

Lisa Jackson's EPA, the Obama administration and mainstream environmental groups such as the Sierra Club clearly agree with that last statement. While they continue to do everything they can to discourage fossil-fuel combustion, they are encouraging biomass combustion. When the EPA released its Boiler MACT rules, it treated biomass combustion far more leniently than fossil-fuel combustion. Boilers that burn biomass have much more lenient emissions limits than those that burn fossil fuels. The Department of Energy and environmental groups have openly supported biomass-combustion projects.

However, because they opened the Pandora's box of obscure and irrelevant secondary environmental risks in the case of fossil-fuel combustion, the left and mainstream environmental groups are beginning to reap what they have sown. The Sierra Club and NRDC and similar organizations have been telling people that combustion (of coal) produces dangerous amounts of air pollutants that will threaten their lives and their children's lives. If this were in fact true in the case of coal, why would one not draw the same conclusion when a power plant burns wood, or a woody grass like miscanthus or switchgrass? Some of the very people who counted on these organizations to tell them the truth have therefore rallied to oppose the biomass energy solution that the Sierra Club advocates.

Consider Dr. William Sammons, a Massachusetts pediatrician who parades around the country pretending to be an expert on biomass combustion and respiratory issues. He is neither. Sammons's expertise is in children's behavioral issues, but he has become a hero to that portion of the populace that has swallowed whole the environmental community's contention that even the tiniest amount of air pollution can cause a grave danger. When Liberty Green LLC proposed to build a small, state-of-the-art power plant that would burn wood in southern Indiana, Sammons popped onto the scene with ridiculous statements that have no scientific validity whatsoever.

"Per unit of power produced, biomass incineration produces more CO_2, more particulates, and more NO_x (nitrogen oxide) than burning coal," Sammons was quoted as saying in *The Bloomington Alternative*. "If allowed to be permitted, the plants in Indiana, as well as the hundreds across the country, will make people sicker and significantly increase health costs while actually accelerating the deterioration of air quality rather than being a solution for climate change."

Any professional who has worked in the environmental industry would be outraged and appalled by such claims. Using biomass for fuel does not introduce CO_2 into the environment; it recycles the compound. Emissions of NO_x and particulates are a function of combustion conditions and add-on controls, not the fuel burned. The assertion that anything related to burning biomass would make people sicker, affect health costs, or deteriorate air quality is ridiculous. The only reason that a gadfly like Sammons would be quoted as a supposed "expert" is that environmental groups have been successful at creating a climate of fear that hopelessly blurs the line between snake oil and science.

Forrest Lucas, the founder of Lucas Oil Products, is one of the big financial backers of the anti-biomass movement. Part of his motivation seems to be that Lucas, a former trucker who pulled himself up by his bootstraps in a classically American success story, is opposed to any sort of government subsidy programs. The biomass industry clearly benefits from some subsidies and tax breaks, so there is merit to that part of Lucas' position for anyone who believes in truly free markets. However, Lucas has also provided support to the people who oppose biomass combustion because of supposed environmental and health risk issues. That is ironic.

Lucas Oil Products manufactures fuel additives and lubricants, thus supporting the continued combustion of fossil fuels in internal-combustion engines. As regulations require continued reductions in the use of fossil fuel to generate electricity, fossil-fuel use in internal-combustion engines—the market that Lucas Oil Products relies upon—continues to grow in relative importance.

The pollutants emitted from a biomass power plant are dispersed over a very wide area because they enter the atmosphere via a very tall smokestack. In contrast, the pollutants emitted from the high compression engines at racetracks across the nation are confined to a relatively small space defined by the limits of the track and grandstand. Spectators at racetracks are exposed, therefore, to a relatively higher concentration of dust, dirt, and toxic emissions while attending the races as compared to the tiny exposures that are the result of fuel combustion in a power plant. You do not believe it? Your nose knows better. If you attend a motor vehicle race of any kind, you are sure to detect the characteristic odors of the race: the fuel, the rubber, the engine exhaust, and all the rest. It is a wonderful smell. However, you can stand as near or as far as you wish from a power plant and you will be hard-pressed to find even the slightest trace of combustion odors.

The sport that Forrest Lucas and his bride love and have so fervently supported is not at all dangerous. Motorsports in America are a wonderful part of our culture. Pointing out the contrasts between the air quality at the average race track and the air quality associated with a power plant is not a matter of impugning the former. Rather, it is about putting the latter in context. If we are unwilling or unable to put combustion in context, then we are doomed to surrender the playing field of public policy to those fanatics who believe that combusting any fuel, in any quantity, with any controls, must be inherently unsafe. Organizations such as Biomass Busters are already working hard to ban wood-burning fireplaces. Backyard barbeques and wood-fired power plants cannot be far behind in their world.

Forty years ago, when power plants and steel mills were belching out plumes of filthy black soot, imagining that we would ever get to this point would have been hard: a moment in time when we have been so successful in cleaning up America that people feel compelled to invent environmental problems to solve. However, that is where we are in 2011. Millions of Americans are out of work, and the nation's industries are struggling to compete in a global market.

The last thing we ought to do is hamstring industry with additional complicated regulations that accomplish virtually nothing. Yet there is so much irrational fear among great swathes of the populace that this is exactly what we are doing. The massive bureaucracy that is the EPA feeds on that fear and, in doing so, empowers its regulators to go wild.

ACKNOWLEDGEMENTS

NO ONE WRITES A BOOK WITHOUT A GREAT DEAL of help and support, and *Regulators Gone Wild* is no exception to that rule. I am grateful to my wonderful wife and sometimes editor Cheryl for her encouragement, patience, understanding, and love. Though writing often takes me away from her side, Cheryl knows how important this part of my life is to me and has always helped me with it. Her advice and ideas have been invaluable in the writing of this book. Likewise my darling daughter Sara, who has put up with her dad's eccentricities for twenty-two years, is a constant source of inspiration and pride. The only joy that comes close to that of raising her has been to watch her mature into a lovely, talented, and brilliant young woman. Thanks, too, to Cheryl's three sons, Alec, Jay and Joseph, for welcoming their mother's strange new husband into their lives.

I am indebted to Randy Petrik, owner and publisher of Examiner Publications, for giving me my first break as a writer and to Tom Phillips, John Farley, and the rest of the Phillips Foundation for moving my career along. The Phillips Foundation has been doing yeoman's work to restore balance to American journalism, and I am very proud to be a Fellow. Many thanks to David Horowitz, Jacob Laskin, Jamie Glazov, Nichole Hungerford, and the rest of the crew at *FrontPage Mag* for helping me take it to the next level. It was Jacob who put me in touch with Encounter Books and Roger Kimball; for that, old buddy, I will always be grateful. Thanks to Roger and his talented, hard-working staff at Encounter for taking a chance on me and this work. They have been a pleasure to work with. And a tip of the hat to the guys and gals at threedonia.com, including Troy, George, Dan, Eric, Mike, BJ, Sondra, and Chuck, along with our wonderful family of readers, who welcomed me into their lives and who have been a constant source of inspiration and encouragement.

Many of the ideas and themes in this book fermented as the result of long discussions over the years with brilliant colleagues. There are too many to mention them all, but a few deserve special attention: Bob Platt, the owner of Mostardi Platt Environmental, who continues to fight the good fight, along with my other friends and colleagues at MPE, including Joe Macak, Lauren Laabs, Roman Plichta, Tim Kinsley, Tom Hiebert, Bruce Meerman, Jim Platt, Dave Ozawa, Scott Banach, and Ken Addison. Other colleagues at other firms were also important in framing my thoughts, including Jim and Linda Huff, Roy Harsch, Renee Cipriano, Kathleen Bassi, Steven Murawski, Nancy Rich, and Bill Anaya.

I chiefly learned critical thinking (a skill much needed in the world today, in my humble opinion) in two venues during my formative years. One was at home, where challenging, raucous debates around the dinner table were a way of life when I was growing up on Chicago's southeast side. My late father, Walter Trzupek, and my late mother, Helen Trzupek, provided that kind of nurturing, intellectually challenging environment, and I will forever be grateful to them both. The same goes for all my siblings, Gene Trzupek, Larry

Trzupek, Ruth Horbaczewki, Dorothy Sliwa, and Gerry Trzupek. They all contributed to this book, directly and indirectly, and they are all very dear to me. I love all you, guys.

The second big influence on my writing career was the two Jesuit institutions that provided me with a high school and college education: St. Ignatius College Prep and Loyola University of Chicago. As a rule of thumb, people who graduate with a degree in chemistry are not expected to pursue a parallel career as a writer. Yet, the Jesuits and other teachers at these two fine institutions provided a classically liberal education that encouraged students to use both sides of their brains at all times. Moreover, they always challenged students to question what they think they know. Teachers such as John Zeunek and James Wall at St. Ignatius, along with Dr. James Wilt and Dr. Janice Mouton at Loyola, were especially influential.

I am not the only one who believes that the EPA and our environmental regulatory structure are out of control. The Heartland Institute is perhaps America's strongest voice for sanity when it comes to battling hyper-regulation, and I appreciate Heartland's encouragement and support as I completed this project. Joe and Diane Bast, Dr. Jay Lehr, and Mike Gemmel are among the many Heartland members to whom I am grateful. Likewise, Steve Milloy, the irrepressible founder of JunkScience.com, remains a source of inspiration, and his site is an invaluable research tool for anyone who questions conventional wisdom. Steve's book *Green Hell* is required reading if you're interested in the environmental movement's methods and goals. With global warming such a hot-button issue today, there are many brave scientists who have dared to question conventional wisdom, and I relied on their work for parts of this book. Among these are Dr. Roy Spencer, Dr. Richard Lindzen, Anthony Watts, Lord Christopher Monckton, Dr. William Gray, Dr. Fred Singer, and Dr. Craig Idso. The work of these brave scientists encouraged me to dig deep, find my own answers, and discover the truth.

Finally, my profound thanks to the hardworking men and women whom it has been my privilege to serve during my primary career as a consultant to industry. These are not faceless corporate executives who make distant decisions in the boardroom. They are instead talented, tireless men and women working on the factory floor who use ingenuity and hard work to provide a living for their fellow employees and prosperity to their country. My job has been to keep the EPA off of their backs so they could continue to do that important work, and it has been an honor to help them. There are too many to name, but among those that I am proud to call both client and friend are Ed Kalebich and Bo Moran at Robbins Community Power; John LaRoi at Vonco Products; Dominick Imburgia, Phyllis Muccianti, Joe Imburgia, and Tim Piper at Packaging Personified; Bob Schultz at Vision Integrated Graphics; Tom Nicolleto, Ben Nguyen, and Roger Darlan at DS Containers; Chuck Tyburk and Bill Tyburk at EnGlobal; and Scott Shaver and Mark Betz at Catalytic Products International. These are the kind of people whose efforts have made America a proud and prosperous nation, and it is my sincere prayer that they and their descendents will continue on this path.

INDEX